Romeo & Juliet

William Shakespeare

A GCSE revision guide
devised and written by Janet Oliver

Contents

Introduction
How to use this book

'Romeo and Juliet' is perhaps the most famous of all love stories. It is packed with drama, romance and violence and has entertained millions of audiences for over four hundred years. Its universal appeal is obvious but tackling such a wide-ranging play in a short exam is a real challenge.

This guide is written and laid out to help you with your revision of 'Romeo and Juliet' and to ensure that your examination response is focused and clear. It is designed to show you how to address the most important elements that the examiner is looking for:

- **language analysis**
- **effective use of quotations**
- **exploration of themes**
- **understanding of character**
- **how an Elizabethan audience would react to the play**

The book is divided into sections of characters and themes with a box at the top of each section which gives a strong, clear overview of the character or theme.

The section is then dealt with using 5-8 key quotations which are in **bold** font. Literary devices are in ***bold italics***.

The analysis of each quotation relates directly to the theme or character. Some of the points are fairly straightforward and some are much more analytical.

The **context** is added at the end to show how it can be woven into an answer with a relevant quotation. Context means the social, historical and literary influences of the time that Shakespeare was writing in and how these are reflected in the play.

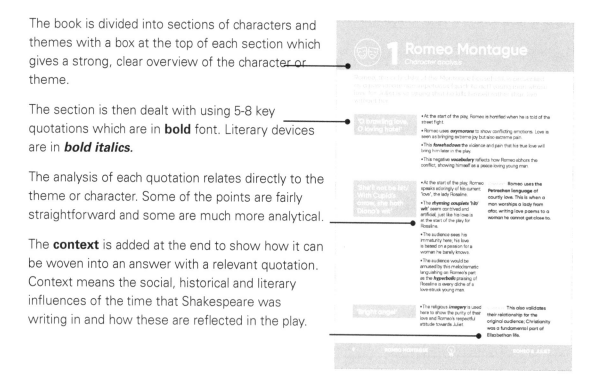

There is also a yellow box entitled 'Grade 9 Exploration' in each chapter. This shows you how you can look at alternative interpretations of the play, which are crucial for gaining a grade of 7 or above.

Look out for the colourful mindmap. It condenses four main points from the chapter, including the Grade 9 Exploration box, into four strands.

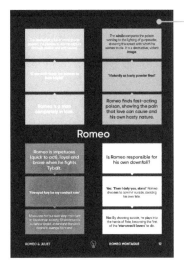

The information is in a shortened format; if you want to keep your revision really focused, use the mind map to make sure you remember the key features of the chapter.

Next comes a sample essay question. This is based on an extract from the play and the question is underneath. Depending on which exam board you are using, the wording will be different but that's fine; the essay question and plan will still be incredibly useful.

The sample essay answer follows. This is based on a 4-5 paragraph formula which answers the question clearly and analytically. The font is small as there is so much detail but, if you are wondering what a top level answer looks like, do read it carefully.

In each chapter, there is a box with essential exam tips: lots of good ideas and reminders that will help you on exam day.

At the back of the book, you will find a handy glossary of all the literary terms with examples and there's a list of the quotations, complete with act and scene references.

Timeline
Plot Summary

The action of 'Romeo and Juliet' takes place in just a few days. The timeline below outlines the key events so that you can see the order in which they take place. The pace of the play is incredibly swift but Shakespeare deliberately keeps the action moving on at a breakneck speed in order to keep the audience fully engaged. The time pressures also mean that characters are forced to make quick, sometimes foolish, decisions which means that the plot keeps developing until the final, tragic ending.

Sunday Morning

- There is a street fight between the men from the Capulet and Montague households.

- Romeo is pining for the love of the unobtainable Rosaline.

Sunday Evening

- Paris asks Lord Capulet for Juliet's hand in marriage and is refused.

- The Capulets have a masked ball which Romeo attends in disguise.

- Tybalt is angry when he sees Romeo but is forbidden to fight by his uncle Lord Capulet.

- Romeo and Juliet meet at the ball and fall instantly in love.

Sunday Night

- Romeo visits Juliet on her balcony and they decide to get married.

Monday Morning

- Romeo persuades Friar Lawrence to perform a marriage ceremony.

- Tybalt sends a challenge to fight Romeo.

- Romeo sends a message to Juliet to meet him at Friar Lawrence's cell.

Monday Afternoon

- Romeo and Juliet are married in secret.

Monday Late Afternoon

- Tybalt kills Mercutio in a fight.

- Romeo kills Tybalt in revenge and is banished by the Prince.

Monday Evening

- Lord Capulet agrees to marry Juliet to Paris.

- Romeo tries to kill himself but the Friar stops this and instead sends Romeo to spend his wedding night with Juliet.

Tuesday Morning

- Romeo says goodbye to Juliet after their wedding night together and heads to Mantua.

- Juliet refuses to marry Paris and visits the Friar for help. He gives her a potion that will make her appear dead and sends Romeo a letter telling him about the plan.

- Returning home, Juliet pretends to agree to the wedding with Paris.

Tuesday Evening

- Preparations take place for the planned wedding of Juliet and Paris.

- Juliet drinks the potion.

Wednesday Morning

- Juliet is discovered as 'dead' and the Capulets bury her in the family tomb.

- Romeo's servant, Balthasar, heads to Mantua and tells Romeo that Juliet is dead. Overcome with grief, Romeo buys poison and travels back to Verona.

Wednesday Night to Thursday Morning

- Romeo arrives at the tomb to find Paris guarding it.

- Paris and Romeo fight and Romeo kills Paris.

- Romeo sees Juliet's 'dead' body and drinks poison.

- Friar Lawrence discovers that Romeo didn't receive the letter and hurries to the tomb to be with Juliet when she wakes.

- Juliet wakes to see the dead body of Romeo. She stabs herself with his sword.

- Everyone arrives at the tomb and the Friar tells the whole sad story.

- United in their joint grief, the Capulets and Montagues make peace.

1 Romeo Montague

Character analysis

Romeo, the only child of the Montague household, is presented as a passionate and impetuous (quick to act) young man whose love for Juliet is so strong that he kills himself rather than live without her.

'O brawling love, O loving hate!'

- At the start of the play, Romeo is horrified when he is told of the street fight.

- Romeo uses **oxymorons** to show conflicting emotions. Love is seen as bringing extreme joy but also extreme pain.

- This **foreshadows** the violence and pain that his true love will bring him later in the play.

- This negative **vocabulary** reflects how Romeo abhors the conflict, showing himself as a peace-loving young man.

'She'll not be hit/ With Cupid's arrow, she hath Diana's wit'

- At the start of the play, Romeo speaks adoringly of his current 'love', the lady Rosaline.

- The **rhyming couplets** 'hit/ wit' seem contrived and artificial, just like his love is at the start of the play for Rosaline.

- The audience sees his immaturity here; his love is based on a passion for a woman he barely knows.

- The audience would be amused by this melodramatic languishing on Romeo's part as the **hyperbolic** praising of Rosaline is every cliche of a love-struck young man.

Context: Romeo uses the **Petrarchan language** of courtly love. This is when a man worships a lady from afar, writing love poems to a woman he cannot get close to.

'bright angel'

- The religious **imagery** is used here to show the purity of their love and Romeo's respectful attitude towards Juliet.

Context: This also validates their relationship for the original audience; Christianity was a fundamental part of Elizabethan life.

• When Romeo first sees Juliet, he falls in love with her beauty. The **metaphor** is a spontaneous outburst of passion which **contrasts** with the earlier artificial declarations of love for Rosaline. Romeo's language is more honest and original and reflects how he is maturing from the opening of the play.

• The **metaphor** is full of emotion; the **plosive 'b'** sounds capture Romeo's passion and enthusiasm.

• It also associates Juliet with light, showing her to be dazzling. Romeo falls in love with Juliet based on her looks; this could be seen as shallow but the intensity of his language convinces the audience that this is genuinely love at first sight and there is a real connection between them.

• The association with Juliet as shining bright is perhaps also negative as it connects Juliet with star **imagery**, reminding us that she, like Romeo, is a **'star-cross'd lover'**, doomed to die.

• In Act 2, Romeo brings his witty joking with Mercutio to an end.

• They have been enjoying a verbal sparring match and the good-humoured banter here shows Romeo to be quick-witted and intelligent. We also see the close friendship between Romeo and Mercutio.

• With Mercutio's death, Romeo is motivated by grief and revenge; here, he is shown to be loyal and brave.

• The **alliteration** of the **'f'** sounds reveals his anger and the reference to **'fire'** captures the heat of his temper - and how destructive this temper will be.

Context: **Elizabethans believed that love made a man effeminate (weak and unmanly). Romeo is here portrayed as aggressive and ready to fight, putting the love that made him weak to one side to avenge his friend's death.**

- When he hears of the 'death' of Juliet, Romeo seeks a swift death himself by drinking deadly poison.

- The intensity of his love is evident as he seeks to kill himself rather than live without Juliet. This impulsive behaviour, acting quickly without thinking things through, ensures that he plays a part in his own death.

- The *simile* compares the poison working to the lighting of gunpowder, showing the speed with which he wishes to die. It is a destructive, violent *image* that shows the pain that love can bring.

- *Structurally*, we are reminded of Friar Lawrence's earlier warning about violent loves culminating (finishing) in violent ends; that prediction is now clearly played out in the apothecary's shop. The relentless progress of fate is evident, as is the violent, doomed nature of his love.

Grade 9 Exploration:
Look at the character in a different way

Does Romeo cause his own downfall?

Yes: Romeo hears about Juliet's death and shouts **'then I defy you, stars!'** He addresses the cold, unfeeling powers that govern his life and cause such grief; he recognises that fate has played its part in Juliet's death but decides to show his own power. By killing himself, he is taking back the last vestige of control, choosing his own place and time of death. Yet if Romeo had not been so hasty, if he had waited just a little while, then tragedy could have been averted. Shakespeare uses the Greek conventions of tragedy which meant that the tragic hero, Romeo, has a hamartia (fatal flaw) which leads to his downfall. It is this fatal flaw of impetuousness that leads to the lovers' deaths.

No: From the beginning, the Prologue warns us that the lovers are **'star-cross'd'** and therefore doomed to die. There is nothing Romeo could do to avert his fate: by choosing suicide as his course of action, he plays into the hands of fate, becoming the first of the **'star-cross'd lovers'** to die.

The Elizabethan audience would have firmly believed in predetermination, that our lives are set out for us by fate. Shakespeare explores in the character of Romeo the idea of self-determination; that our own decisions and choices have clear consequences.

Essential Exam Tips

☑ Make at least three separate points based on the extract.

☑ When writing about the play as a whole, refer to at least three other parts of the text.

The **metaphor** is full of emotion and passion; the **plosive** 'b' sounds capture Romeo's passion and enthusiasm.

The **simile** compares the poison working to the lighting of gunpowder, showing the speed with which he wishes to die. It is a destructive, violent **image**.

'O she doth teach the torches to burn bright!'

'violently as hasty powder fired'

Romeo is a man completely in love.

Romeo finds fast-acting poison, showing the pain that love can cause and his own hasty nature.

Romeo

Romeo is loyal and brave when he fights Tybalt.

Is Romeo responsible for his own downfall?

'fire-eyed fury be my conduct now'

Yes: 'Then I defy you, stars!' Romeo chooses to commit suicide, deciding his own fate.

Masculine honour was very important in Elizabethan society; Shakespeare's audience would understand Romeo's desire to avenge his friend.

No: By choosing suicide, he plays into the hands of Fate, becoming the first of the **'star-cross'd lovers'** to die.

Sample GCSE Exam Question

Read the following extract from Act 1 Scene 5 of 'Romeo and Juliet'. Answer the questions that follow.

At this point in the play, Romeo is at Lord Capulet's party and has just seen Juliet.

ROMEO:
O, she doth teach the torches to burn bright!
It seems she hangs upon the cheek of night
Like a rich jewel in an Ethiope's ear;
Beauty too rich for use, for earth too dear!
So shows a snowy dove trooping with crows,
As yonder lady o'er her fellows shows.
The measure done, I'll watch her place of stand,
And, touching hers, make blessed my rude hand.
Did my heart love till now? forswear it, sight!
For I ne'er saw true beauty till this night.

a) Discuss how Romeo is presented in this extract.

b) Discuss how Romeo is presented in the play as a whole.

 # Sample GCSE Exam Answer

 Start with an overview

Romeo, the only child of the Montague household, is presented as a passionate and impetuous young man whose love for Juliet is so strong that he kills himself rather than live without her. In the extract, the audience watches him fall deeply in love with the daughter of his family's enemy, setting in motion the chain of events that leads to the tragic end of the play.

✔ Focus on how Romeo is a passionate and romantic man

In this scene, we are presented with a young man who is intense and romantic, a man caught up in the joy of new love. The *metaphor* **'she doth teach the torches to burn bright!'** is full of emotion; the *plosive* **'b'** sounds capture Romeo's passion and enthusiasm. The *alliteration* of the 't' also shows his excitement, as does the *exclamatory* **'O'**, as if the words are spontaneously pouring out of his soul. The *simile* **'it seems she hangs upon the cheek of night/ Like a rich jewel in an Ethiope's ear'** continues the association of Juliet with light. This is a positive *image* showing her to be dazzling, and the light is a *symbol* of hope and warmth; no wonder Romeo is falling so completely in love.

 Make the point that Romeo could be seen as fickle (changeable)

We might question the validity of this love and see Romeo as a shallow, fickle young man as he asks himself **'did my heart love till now? forswear it, sight!'** The audience would perhaps be amused by this as, only hours earlier, he was declaring undying love for Rosaline. At the start of the play, Romeo is presented as immature as he sighs over Rosaline, saying **'she'll not be hit/With Cupid's arrow, she hath Diana's wit'**. The *rhyming couplets* seem contrived and artificial and the audience sees his immaturity here, his love based on a passion for a woman he barely knows. He relies heavily on the traditional *Petrarchan language* of courtly love, when a man worships a lady from afar, writing love poems to a woman he cannot get close to. The style sounds artificial, just like Romeo's love for Rosaline is. The audience would be amused by this melodramatic languishing on Romeo's part as the **hyperbolic** praising of Rosaline reflects every cliche of a love-struck young man. However, although the abandonment of Rosaline for Juliet seems like a sudden change, the honesty and maturity of his language in this extract shows us how this new love is genuine.

✔ Make the point that Romeo is humble and respectful

Romeo is presented as humble, seeing himself as profane (not religious) and Juliet as sacred and superior to him. He says that by touching her he will **'make blessed my rude hand'**, therefore improving himself and blessing himself with her shining goodness. This **contrast** of the profane and the religious reflects one of the themes of the play: that of opposing forces in conflict that need to be reconciled in order for peace to come to Verona. Here, love is seen as a force for good, changing Romeo for the better. The Christian religion was a fundamental part of Elizabethan England and the religious language here validates the pure nature of Romeo and Juliet's love. This means that when the lovers commit suicide, seen as a serious sin by the Church, the audience still has sympathy for them.

✔ Move to the point that Romeo is impetuous

Romeo is impetuous, falling in love and making plans in an instant. He does not stop to consider the possible consequences of his actions but says **'I'll watch her place of stand'**, the **modal verb** 'will' reflecting his determination and quick decisiveness. This impetuousness is seen in Act 3 when Mercutio dies and Romeo is motivated by grief and revenge, crying **'fire-eyed fury be my conduct now'**. The reference to **'fire'** shows the heat of his temper and how destructive his inability to control his emotions will be. Elizabethans believed that love made a man effeminate (weak and unmanly) yet Romeo is here seen as aggressive and ready to fight, putting the love that made him weak to one side to avenge his friend's death. His fierce loyalty is understandable, especially to an Elizabethan audience which placed high value on masculine honour. Yet this loyalty ultimately leads to his death.

✔ Explore whether Romeo was to blame for his own death

Romeo's death is inevitable from the moment that he hears about Juliet's death and shouts **'then I defy you, stars!'** He addresses the cold, unfeeling powers that govern his life and cause such grief; he recognises that fate has played its part in Juliet's death but decides to show his own power. By killing himself, he is taking back the last vestige of control, choosing his own place and time of death. Yet if Romeo had not been so hasty, if he had waited just a little while, then tragedy could have been averted. Shakespeare follows the Greek conventions of tragedy which means that the tragic hero (Romeo) has a **hamartia** (fatal flaw) which leads to his downfall. It is this fatal flaw of impetuousness that leads to the lovers' deaths. However, it is perhaps unfair to blame Romeo at all. From the beginning, the Prologue warns us that the lovers are **'star-cross'd'** and therefore doomed to die. There is nothing Romeo could do to avert his fate: by choosing suicide as his course of action, he plays into the hands of fate, becoming the first of the **'star-cross'd lovers'** to die. The Elizabethan audience would have firmly believed in predetermination, that our lives are set out for us by fate. Shakespeare explores in the character of Romeo the idea of self-determination, that our own decisions and choices allow us control over our lives. Yet whether or not we believe him to be culpable (to blame) for the tragedy, almost all audiences cannot fail to warm to the passionate, witty and loyal character that is Romeo.

2 Juliet Capulet
Character analysis

Juliet, the only child of the Capulet household, is a character whose love for Romeo changes her from an obedient girl to a passionate young woman.

'not fourteen'	• Juliet is very young. Shakespeare makes her this age to heighten the sense of tragedy, that someone so young and innocent can die for love.

'Madam, I am here. What is your will?'

• Juliet addresses her mother formally, showing that she is distant from her mother.

• The question **'what is your will?'** establishes her as compliant and docile (obedient), politely obeying her mother.

Context: Children were brought up by servants in the 14th century and the relationships between parents and children would often have been formal. Girls were expected to obey their parents at this time.

'If he be married / My grave is like to be my wedding bed'

• When Juliet meets Romeo, she falls deeply in love, reflecting how youthful and passionate she is.

• Her language is extreme; she will die if she cannot marry Romeo. She, like Romeo, has been swept up in a storm of strong emotion, showing the intensity of true love.

• Shakespeare uses **foreshadowing**; the association here of love with death reminds us of the Prologue's warning that these lovers are **'star-cross'd'** and so doomed to die.

• We could question the suddenness and authenticity of this very new love but the **structure** of the play allows us, the audience, to intimately (closely) watch the unfolding of love between the two. This enables us to understand the strength of their emotions which affects their decision making.

• We also suspend our disbelief, overlooking the implausible (unbelievable) elements in the narrative. The fast pace of the play does not give us time to pause and question just how genuine their love for one another is.

'bright angel'

- Romeo's language defines Juliet with light *imagery*, capturing the shining quality of Juliet.

- The light *imagery* emphasises her physical beauty as it illustrates just how dazzling she is. She is seen as a force for the good as light is also a symbol of hope; the *imagery* reflects her personality in an incredibly positive way.

- Yet the association with Juliet as shining bright is perhaps negative as it connects Juliet with star *imagery*, reminding the audience that she is a **'star-cross'd lover'**, doomed to die.

Context: **This religious *imagery* shows that Juliet is seen as pure and almost sacred; it also validates their relationship for the Elizabethan audience, to whom the Christian religion was a fundamental part of their lives.**

'too rash, too unadvised, too sudden'

- Juliet questions the intensity and wisdom of their love, suggesting that she is more cautious and more mature than the headstrong (impatient) Romeo.

- She is aware of the possible consequences of their love, and the *tri-colon* here reminds Romeo, and the audience, of the many negatives to their love. It is not straightforward and could, and indeed will, be dangerous. The *tri-colon* piles on the many negatives of their love and captures Juliet's anxiety.

'Spread thy close curtain, love-performing night'

- Juliet is impatient for night-time as she waits for her husband on their wedding night. The *imperative verb* **'spread'** (or 'close') highlights Juliet's eagerness for her wedding night.

- We see her here as passionate and hot-blooded, full of desire for her new husband. The *soliloquy* shows her development from the beginning of the play, when, shy and demure, she waited on her parents' pleasure. Here, she is seeking her own pleasure and the *command verb* reflects this control she has taken over her own life.

Context: **Juliet's sexuality is clearly shown here, safely shown, as she is now married. Sex outside marriage would be outside the boundaries of acceptable behaviour in the Elizabethan era but, because she is married, Shakespeare can now show her sexual side.**

- Juliet claims that she will kill herself rather than marry Paris and her **_hyperbole_** reveals her complete horror at dishonouring her husband. Her love for Romeo is absolute and she proves herself true and loyal in her declaration of choosing to die rather than betray him.

- The **_dramatic irony_** here is painful; we know that she does indeed die for love, showing her courage and dedication. Yet again, Shakespeare is reminding the audience of the Prologue's warning that she will take her life; we watch her make her desperate plans, painfully aware that she is powerless to escape her tragic fate.

Grade 9 Exploration:
Look at the character in a different way

Does Juliet deserve our full sympathy?

Yes: Juliet's suicide is an incredibly painful moment for the audience as the lively, passionate girl dies for love, and audiences have enormous sympathy for her. She does deceive her family by faking her death but this deceit is only a consequence of the situation the incredibly young and naive Juliet finds herself in, and her actions reflect her love and commitment to her husband. The action of the play only lasts five days and this whirlwind speed forces Juliet to make hasty decisions. The audience, also caught up in the fast-moving action of the play, feels empathy for the innocent girl who is so completely and helplessly in love.

No: Juliet is highly manipulative when she fakes her own death, causing huge distress to her already grieving family. This shows a devious side to her character and perhaps makes us doubt her integrity. This sly side to her character is also seen in Act 1 when her mother asks her to **'like'** of Paris' love and Juliet replies **'I'll look to like, if looking liking move'**. Her slick mirroring of her mother's words suggests a sharp intelligence which buys her time; she does not commit herself but instead prevaricates. She is not so much innocent as a girl adept at manipulation.

As a young girl in fourteenth century Italy, and sixteenth century England, Juliet would have had very little power. These patriarchal (male-dominated) societies would have left her, a young girl, with no option but to plot and deceive.

The formal question suggests that she is distant from her mother.

Children were brought up by servants in the 14th century; girls were expected to be humble and docile.

She is aware of the possible consequences of their love, and the **tri-colon** here reminds Romeo, and the audience, of the many negatives to their love. Their love is dangerous.

'Madam, what is your will?'

'too rash, too unadvised, too sudden'

Juliet begins the play as meek and obedient, politely and formally addressing her mother.

Juliet is more mature and cautious than Romeo.

Juliet

Juliet changes to become more confident and assertive.

Does Juliet deserve our full sympathy?

'Spread thy close curtain'

Yes: Her actions are the result of youth and inexperience. As a young girl without any power in 14th century Italy, she would have had little choice other than to lie and deceive.

The **imperative verb** shows Juliet's impatience for her wedding night; we see her here as passionate and hot-blooded, full of desire for her new husband.

No: Juliet is deceitful, faking her own death and manipulating her parents to her own advantage.

Sample GCSE Exam Question

Read the following extract from Act 3 Scene 2 of 'Romeo and Juliet'. Answer the questions that follow.

At this point in the play, Juliet is waiting for her wedding night.

JULIET:
Come, gentle night, come, loving, black-brow'd night,
Give me my Romeo; and, when he shall die,
Take him and cut him out in little stars,
And he will make the face of heaven so fine
That all the world will be in love with night
And pay no worship to the garish sun.
O, I have bought the mansion of a love,
But not possess'd it, and, though I am sold,
Not yet enjoy'd: so tedious is this day
As is the night before some festival
To an impatient child that hath new robes
And may not wear them.

a) Discuss how Juliet is presented in this extract.

b) Discuss how Juliet is presented in the play as a whole.

 # Sample GCSE Exam Answer

 Start with an overview

Juliet, the only child of the Capulet household, is a character whose love for Romeo changes her from an obedient girl to a passionate young woman. In this extract, Juliet waits for her wedding night with eagerness, demonstrating the power of love to evoke strong emotions and alter personalities.

 **Focus on how Juliet is presented as a girl excited at the thought of enjoying her wedding night**

In the extract, Juliet instructs the night to come quickly in the line **'come, gentle night, come, loving, black-brow'd night'**. The *repetition* of the *imperative verb* **'come'** higlights Juliet's impatience for Romeo to join her in the marriage bed. We see her here as passionate and hot-blooded, full of desire for her new husband. Here, she is seeking her own pleasure and the **command verbs** demonstrate this control she has taken over her own life. Her impatience reminds us that she is a girl in the grips of first love, emphasising her young age. The secrecy of their relationship is emphasised by the **personification** of night, sheltering and protecting the lovers in its **'black-brow'd'** darkness. We are reminded that the lovers need secrecy to be safe; this creates an uneasy feeling, especially **juxtaposed** with the high drama and violence of the previous fight scene. Juliet's sexuality is clearly displayed here, safely displayed, as she is now married. Sex outside marriage would be outside the boundaries of acceptable behaviour in the Elizabethan era but, because she is married, Shakespeare can now explore her sexual side.

Develop this point that Juliet is a young girl in love

Juliet's great love for Romeo is evident in the *metaphor* **'when he shall die/Take him and cut him out in little stars'**. Stars were seen as eternal and so reflect how deeply she loves Romeo, wanting him to exist forever, while the beautiful use of light *imagery* shows us how dazzling she finds her husband. *Foreshadowing* is used here to remind the audience what we know from the Prologue, that Romeo, as a **'star-cross'd lover'**, is doomed to die. We know from the violence of the previous scene (the deaths of Mercutio and Tybalt) that death is ever-present and we feel uneasy as Juliet talks of his death. We know that she and Romeo are doomed and that her youthful happiness will be short-lived, but are powerless to stop the course of fate.

✔ Make the point that Juliet is seen as a force for good

Juliet associates Romeo with heaven when she says **'he will make the face of heaven so fine'**. When the couple first meet, Romeo sees himself as profane (not religious) and Juliet as pure and sacred. He calls her **'bright angel'**, using religious language to show her perfection, and Romeo improves himself and blesses himself when he touches Juliet's hand when he first meets her. This demonstrates the conflict between the profane and the sacred in the play which is reconciled now they are married and so have the blessing of the Church. With Juliet's religious language showing how Romeo will brighten heaven, Romeo has also become sacred and this conflict is resolved. Yet their union is very short-lived, perhaps suggesting how other forces in conflict with each other still conspire to destroy the couple.

✔ Make the point that Juliet is a character who changes

At the start of the play, Juliet addresses her mother formally, **'madam, I am here. What is your will?'**, showing that she is distant from her mother. The question **'what is your will?'** establishes her as compliant and docile (obedient), politely obeying her mother. Noble children were brought up by servants in the fourteenth century and relationships between parents and children were often formal. Girls were expected to obey their parents at this time. Juliet's personality develops when she meets Romeo, showing the changing power of love. Yet even on the balcony scene, she displays a more cautious attitude than Romeo, saying their love is **'too rash, too unadvised, too sudden'**. This exemplifies her maturity as she is aware of the possible consequences of their love. The anxiety captured in this *tri-colon* here reminds Romeo, and the audience, of the many negatives to their love. It is not straightforward and could, and indeed will, be dangerous.

✔ Explore whether Juliet has our full sympathy

Later, Juliet claims that she will kill herself rather than marry Paris, that she will '**leap... from the battlements'**. Her *hyperbole* captures her complete horror at dishonouring her husband. Her love for Romeo is absolute and she proves herself true and loyal in her declaration of dying rather than betray him. The *dramatic irony* here is painful; we know that she does indeed die for love, proving her courage and dedication. Yet there is another side to Juliet; she is highly manipulative when she fakes her own death, causing huge distress to her already grieving family. This shows a devious side to her character and perhaps makes us doubt her integrity. This sly side to her character is also seen in Act 1 when her mother asks her to **'like'** of Paris' love and Juliet replies **'I'll look to like, if looking liking move'**. Her slick mirroring of her mother's words suggests a sharp intelligence which buys her time; she does not commit herself but instead prevaricates. However, this view of her is perhaps unfair; her deceitful actions simply show the lengths that Juliet is driven to. As a young girl in fourteenth century Italy, she would have had very little power; this patriarchal society would have left her, a young girl, with no option but to plot and deceive. In the end, it is hard not to agree with the Prince when he tells the audience that **'never was a story of more woe than this of Juliet and her Romeo'**, and we feel the pain of the death of the young, passionate Juliet Capulet.

3 The Nurse
Character analysis

The Nurse is a warm, affectionate character who is close to Juliet and a favoured servant in the Capulet household. Shakespeare uses her in part as a comic character and in part as a *plot device*.

'I am weary, give me leave a while'

- When the Nurse returns from meeting Romeo, she teases Juliet by pretending to be tired, delaying telling her of the marriage plans.

- This illustrates her playful nature as it drags out the scene for the impatient Juliet. This entertains the audience who, of course, know about the plans; we are in the position of knowing what Juliet doesn't.

- Shakespeare uses the Nurse here as a *plot device* to create humour.

'O honey nurse'

- Juliet addresses the Nurse with deep affection; the *epithet* here shows that she sees her Nurse as sweet and warm.

- It is a very different relationship to the one with her mother which is much more formal; Juliet addresses her mother as '**madam**', a stilted (awkward), distant title that is far removed from the warmth of '**honey nurse**'.

- The Nurse displays equal affection to Juliet, calling her '**ladybird**'.

Context: **At the time, children in noble households would be brought up by servants. A distant relationship between mother and daughter would not have been unusual while the job of wet-nursing (breast-feeding) was often given to women of low birth. No wonder Juliet and the Nurse have a close bond, formed from the early days of breastfeeding and the constant time spent together.**

'You shall bear the burden soon at night'

- Nurse uses **puns**, making crude sexual reference to Juliet's wedding night.

- Shakespeare uses the Nurse as a **contrast** to the purity of the young lovers' feelings for each other, showing the physical side to love.

Context: **Shakespeare's original audience would have enjoyed the play on words and the bawdy humour. In the theatre, the audience would have been standing in front of the stage, fidgeting and chatting, so humour would have been a device to hold their attention.**

'You are to blame, my lord, to rate her so'

- When Juliet defies her father, the Nurse tries to defend Juliet to Lord Capulet, demonstrating her loyalty to Juliet. Yet she is quickly silenced, terrified of Capulet's fury.

'Beshrew my very heart, I think you are happy in this second match'

- The Nurse advises Juliet to forget her husband, Romeo, and obey her parents by marrying Paris.

- This shows an incredible practicality and also a shocking lack of consistency; the Nurse is very quick to forget that Juliet has left her bridal bed only moments before. Again, Shakespeare uses the fickle (disloyal) Nurse as a contrast to highlight the true, steadfast love of Romeo and Juliet.

- ' **Beshrew**' means 'curse' and the Nurse **repeats** the phrase, **foreshadowing** the end of the play. Shakespeare reminds us of the dark tragedy waiting to unfold; with the death of the lovers and the discovery of the secret marriage, the nurse will indeed be cursed at the end: punished emotionally for losing her little girl and punished physically as is implied by the Prince in Act 5.

Context: **Bigamy (marrying two people at the same time) was a serious sin in the eyes of the Church and the law. The Nurse's advice to commit bigamy would affect her standing with an Elizabethan audience, to whom the Christian religion was a fundamental part of their lives.**

- The Nurse reacts with violent grief to the discovery of Juliet's body. The **repetition** and **hyperbole** reflect her great distress at the death of the girl she has loved since a newborn.

- The Nurse is usually garrulous (talkative) so it's an indication of how distraught (upset) she is that she is so limited with her words.

Grade 9 Exploration:
Look at the character in a different way

Does the Nurse truly love Juliet?

No: She lets Juliet down at her time of need, unwilling to defend her to Lord Capulet. The endearments she uses for Juliet are of a flighty, light-hearted nature such as '**lamb/ladybird**' and she is clearly a fickle (changeable) character, praising Romeo and then damning him in rapid succession. We wonder whether she even truly knows Juliet as a character as she speaks of Juliet in terms of her beauty as **'the prettiest babe'**, which is a shallow way of defining her. The Nurse seems to place high value on the status she is given as Juliet's servant; when she goes to meet Romeo, she puts on pretentious airs, asking for her **'fan'** from another servant, making us wonder whether she only loves Juliet as a pretty doll and in terms of her own advantage and position. This is borne out by the **hyperbole** she uses when Juliet's body is discovered: **'O day O day O hateful day!'** which is very **repetitive**, very dramatic and very similar in style to the hysterical words she uses over Tybalt's death. She in unlikely to have cared for Tybalt in the same way as she did Juliet which makes her reaction to Juliet's death seem false.

Yes: There is real distress evident in the **repetition** of **'O day O day!'**; she, who is so garrulous (talkative), is reduced to **repeating** the same phrase, showing her genuine grief. In Act 3, she does not defend Juliet more vigorously when Juliet defies her father because her own power is so limited.

As the Nurse is only a servant in a noble household in the 14th century, Capulet's terrible rage would have reminded her of her own lack of power. Her part in the deception would have been severely punished by her master and this fear of punishment influences her behaviour.

Essential Exam Tips

☑ **Don't worry if there are words/phrases in the extract that you don't understand. Ignore these and focus on the parts that you do understand.**

☑ **Spend 5 minutes planning your answer; this helps you organise your ideas into a structure that is clear for the examiner.**

The *adjective* 'honey' shows the Nurse as a warm, sweet character, revealing the affection between the Nurse and Juliet.

This bawdy (rude) joke about sex on Juliet's wedding night serves two purposes: 1) entertainment 2) it *contrasts* with the pure romantic love of Romeo and Juliet.

'O honey nurse'

'You shall bear the burden soon at night'

The Nurse has a close, loving relationship with Juliet.

Shakespeare uses the Nurse as a comic character to amuse the audience.

The Nurse

The Nurse lets Juliet down by advising her to forget Romeo and obey her parents by marrying Paris.

Does the Nurse truly love Juliet?

'Beshrew my very heart, I think you are happy in this second match'

Yes: ' O day, O day, O hateful day!' The *repetition* and *hyperbole* reflect her distress at Juliet's death.

The Nurse is fickle (changeable). '**Beshrew**' means to curse, and the Nurse *repeats* this, *foreshadowing* the tragedy that will unfold.

No: The Nurse defines Juliet by her beauty, as '**the prettiest babe**' which is a very shallow way of defining her.

Sample GCSE Exam Question

Read the following extract from Act 1 Scene 3 of 'Romeo and Juliet'.

Answer both questions below the text.

At this point in the play, Lady Capulet is trying to talk to Juliet about a possible marriage but the Nurse interrupts with a story of Juliet as a baby.

LADY CAPULET:
Enough of this; I pray thee, hold thy peace.
NURSE:
Yes, madam: yet I cannot choose but laugh,
To think it should leave crying and say 'Ay.'
And yet, I warrant, it had upon its brow
A bump as big as a young cockerel's stone;
A parlous knock; and it cried bitterly:
'Yea,' quoth my husband, 'fall'st upon thy face?
Thou wilt fall backward when thou comest to age;
Wilt thou not, Jule?' it stinted and said 'Ay.'
JULIET:
And stint thou too, I pray thee, nurse, say I.
NURSE:
Peace, I have done. God mark thee to his grace!
Thou wast the prettiest babe that e'er I nursed.

a) Write about how the Nurse is presented in this extract.

b) Write about how the Nurse is presented in the play as a whole.

Sample GCSE Exam Answer

☑ Start with an overview

The Nurse is a warm, affectionate character who is close to Juliet and a favoured servant in the Capulet household. Shakespeare uses her in part as a comic character and in part as a ***plot device***. In the extract, she dominates the conversation, establishing her as a lively and entertaining character.

☑ Make the point that the Nurse has a privileged position in the Capulet household

Even though she's been instructed to be quiet, the Nurse continues with an ***anecdote*** about Juliet when she was a toddler, replying **'yes, madam: yet I cannot choose but laugh'**. There is token respect in the title **'madam'** and a semblance of compliance in the **'yes'**. However, the ***conjunction* 'yet'** shows how the Nurse ignores the instruction to be quiet as she ploughs on with her ***anecdote***. She is clearly a determined character and one who has a privileged position in the Capulet household. Her long rambling story establishes her as a garrulous (talkative) character and the story also prevents the frustrated Lady Capulet from talking to Juliet which is amusing for the audience. Shakespeare is using her as a comic device to add humour to the play.

☑ Develop this point that the Nurse is a comic character

The Nurse ends her story with Juliet who **'will fall backward'** which suggests her lying down to have sex.

Her bawdy humour is often evident in the play, such as when she refers to Juliet's wedding night with the pun **'you shall bear the burden soon at night'**. Shakespeare uses the Nurse as a **contrast** to the purity of the young lovers' feelings for each other, illustrating the physical side to love. Shakespeare's original audience would have enjoyed the play on words and the bawdy (sexual) humour. In the theatre, the audience would have been standing in front of the stage, fidgeting and chatting, so humour would have been a device to hold their attention.

☑ Make the point that the Nurse has affection for Juliet

The tone of the Nurse's story is of warm affection with the detail of the **'bump as big as a young cockerel's stone'** showing how the memory is a vivid one for the Nurse, and this love comes from the fact that she **'nursed'** Juliet as a baby. A distant relationship between a noble mother and daughter would not have been unusual in Elizabethan society while the job of wet-nursing (breast-feeding) was often given to women of low birth. No wonder Juliet and the Nurse have a close bond, formed from the early days of breastfeeding and the constant time spent together, and we see this in the way the Nurse blesses Juliet, saying **'God mark thee to his grace!'** Her love for Juliet is evident and Juliet returns it in full, demonstrating her affection elsewhere in the play with the **epithet 'honey nurse'** which shows that Juliet sees her Nurse as sweet and warm. This close relationship also allows Shakespeare to use the Nurse as a **plot device**; her position as Juliet's servant means that she has the freedom to meet with Romeo and arrange the secret wedding.

☑ Make the point that the Nurse betrays Juliet

Early on in the play, the Nurse is established as Juliet's confidante and so we are shocked when the Nurse betrays Juliet in Act 3, advising Juliet to forget her husband and obey her parents by marrying Paris: **'beshrew my very heart, I think you are happy in this second match.'** This shows an incredible practicality and also a shocking lack of consistency; the Nurse is very quick to forget that Juliet has left her bridal bed only moments before. Again, Shakespeare uses the fickle (disloyal) Nurse as a **contrast** to highlight the true, solid love of Romeo and Juliet. While the Nurse advises a neat solution to the problem, Juliet would rather **'leap from the battlements'** than betray Romeo by marrying another. **'Beshrew'** means 'curse' and the Nurse **repeats** the phrase, **foreshadowing** the end of the play. Shakespeare reminds us of the dark tragedy waiting to unfold for, with the death of the lovers and the discovery of the secret marriage, the Nurse will indeed be cursed at the end: punished emotionally for losing her little girl and punished physically as is implied by the Prince in Act 5. This punishment could be regarded as deserved; bigamy (marrying two people at the same time) was a serious sin in the eyes of the Church. The Nurse's advice would affect her standing with an Elizabethan audience, to whom the Christian religion was a fundamental part of their lives.

☑ The Nurse's character is open to interpretation by audiences

In this extract, the Nurse defines Juliet by her beauty, calling her the **'prettiest babe'** and elsewhere calls her **'ladybird'** and **'lamb'**. These are lighthearted endearments of little substance and suggest a surface rather than a deep affection. The Nurse seems to place high value on the status she is given as Juliet's servant; when she goes to meet Romeo, she puts on pretentious airs, asking for her **'fan'** from another servant. Perhaps she only loves Juliet as a pretty doll and in terms of her own advantage and position. This is borne out by the **hyperbole** she uses when Juliet's body is discovered **'O day O day O hateful day!'**- very **repetitive**, very dramatic and very similar in style to the hysterical words she uses over Tybalt's death. She is unlikely to have cared for Tybalt in the same way as she did Juliet which makes her reaction to Juliet's death seem rather false. We also see her betray Juliet twice, once by failing to defend her when she is under attack from her father and also when she encourages Juliet to marry Paris. Yet this view of her is perhaps unfair. There is real distress evident in the **repetition** of **'O day O day!'**; she, who is so garrulous (talkative), is reduced to repeating the same phrase, showing her genuine grief. Furthermore, she does not defend Juliet more vigorously as she is only a servant in a noble household in the fourteenth century and Capulet's terrible rage would have reminded her of her own lack of power. Her part in the deception would have been heavily punished by her master and this fear of punishment influences her behaviour. Overall, whether we blame the Nurse for her part in the tragedy or not, there is little doubt that her warm humour enhances the play and that her character is a truly memorable one.

Friar Lawrence is the religious figure who acts as counsellor to the young lovers, enabling the audience to hear the plans as they are being made. His knowledge of herbs means that he is useful as a *plot device* in moving the story along.

'day/night' 'baleful weeds/ precious-juiced flowers'

- Shakespeare presents us with a holy man who is linked with nature. The setting is **'outside'**, presumably in a garden, collecting healing herbs so that we see him in a positive light as someone in touch with nature.

- This is also a *plot device*; his association with herbs early on means that the audience later implicitly (completely) believes the plot of the herbal potion giving Juliet the appearance of death.

- Shakespeare creates a *semantic field* of opposing contrasts **'day/night' 'weeds/ flowers**' which highlights one of the themes: that of conflict and clashes and the need to reconcile (bring together) opposing forces.

Context: **Elizabethan audiences had faith in religious authority and a belief in the natural order; the Friar's connection with both of these (his monk's robe and 'basket' of herbs) establishes him as a person who can be trusted.**

'pupil mine/ young son'

- The Friar is a teacher and the *possessive pronoun* 'mine' captures his closeness to Romeo. The Friar and Romeo also later share *rhyming couplets*, reflecting the bond between them.

- This bond is also shown in the words **'young son'**. Romeo confides in the Friar when he cannot talk to his actual father. The feud between Capulets and Montagues ensures that Romeo and Juliet are unable to talk to their families and therefore seek advice elsewhere. This means they act in secret, which plays its part in the tragic end.

Context: **At this time, religious figures were often involved in the education of young noble children. A formality in the relationship between parents and children was normal so it would have been customary for children to turn to characters such as Friar Lawrence and the Nurse for comfort, support and guidance.**

'Turn your households' rancour to pure love'

- There is a clear **statement** of intent here; the Friar wants the love of Romeo and Juliet to act as a way of healing the rift (divide) between the two houses. He is seen as a healer from the beginning and his reasons for trying to help them are for the greater good of Verona and to put an end to the violence. His **contrasting words** 'rancour' (meaning 'animosity/dislike') to **'love'** highlights one of the themes of the play, that of conflict and the need to bring balance and harmony.

- It is ironic that the lovers' marriage does ensure an end to the rivalry but through death, certainly not as the Friar planned. This demonstrates how fate cannot be controlled and changed.

'These violent delights have violent ends'

- Even the lovers' wedding day is underscored with references to death. Friar Lawrence's words here warn of the explosive nature of love; the **repetition** of the word **'violent'** issues a warning to the characters and to us. Despite knowing these dangers, he still marries the lovers and an audience might question whether this is a responsible action of an older man in a position of authority.

- **Structurally**, we remember this warning later in the play when Romeo seeks a death as swift and **'violently as hasty powder fired'**. As the warning is proved to be true, the audience sees the relentless progress of fate and understands the violent, doomed nature of this love.

'Holy Church incorporate two as one'

- The Friar's last words of the wedding scene are that of unity and harmony. The blessing of the church is given to the lovers and their relationship is now within the safe boundaries of the church. However, even this is not enough to ward off the evil fate that awaits them.

- The wedding is important in terms of **structure**; the next scene is that of the hot, steamy afternoon in Verona when tempers run high and Mercutio and Tybalt are killed. This sharply **contrasts** with the peaceful scene of the wedding where the Friar plays his role of being associated with peace and harmony.

'I dare no longer stay'

- At the end, the Friar's wisdom is replaced by naked fear as he deserts Juliet in the tomb.

- Like the Nurse, he betrays Juliet; he fails in his responsibility to her as her counsellor and mentor.

'unkind hour'

- The Friar blames fate for the tragic events which means that he washes his hands of any guilt.

- He sees it as fate's cruel predestination that the lovers are dead and therefore he is not to blame for the tragedy.

Context: **The Elizabethan audience would have firmly believed in predetermination, that our lives are set out for us by fate. The Friar's excuses would have been understood by Shakespeare's original audience.**

Grade 9 Exploration:
Look at the character in a different way

Is the Friar a 'good' man?

Yes: He is acknowledged as a '**holy man**' by the Prince. This validation of his character by the Prince, the most senior figure in the play, guides our response to see him as a man with good intentions. His only motivation is to reconcile the two warring families through the marriage of Romeo and Juliet; he has a deep and genuine desire to reconcile the opposing forces which have caused so much bloodshed in Verona and his constant references to opposites reflect his desire to heal the conflict.

No: His actions are irresponsible, especially to an Elizabethan audience who were very accustomed to marriages being made through parents, not secretly and without parental consent. In the Catholic society of 14th century Verona, the Friar has enormous power and he abuses this power. There is perhaps a sense that his belief in his own power allows him to play at God, giving Juliet the potion that will slow her heart and make her seem as dead; he is meddling with lives with disastrous consquences. Yet this power quickly ebbs away in the Capulets' tomb and he is eager to blame fate rather than take much responsibility for the events.

Essential Exam Tips

☑ Keep quotations short and focused; don't copy out big chunks.

☑ Try to embed quotations (see sample essay on the next page)

The **possessive pronoun** 'mine' shows his closeness to Romeo. The Friar and Romeo also share **rhyming couplets**, reflecting the bond between them.

The **semantic field** of opposing contrasts highlights one of the themes of the play- that of conflict and clashes and the need to reconcile opposing forces.

'Pupil mine/young son'

'baleful weeds/precious-juiced flowers'

The Friar is close to Romeo, acting as counsellor.

The Friar is a healer, working with nature.

Friar Lawrence

The Friar blames fate, not himself, for the tragedy.

Should we view the Friar in a positive or negative light?

'unkind hour'

Positive: His only motivation in the play is to reconcile the two warring families: **'turn your households' rancour to pure love'**.

The Elizabethan audience would have firmly believed in predetermination, that our lives are set out for us by fate.

Negative: He was fully aware of the possible disastrous outcomes of passionate love, even warning Romeo that **'violent delights have violent ends'**. He is irresponsible.

Sample GCSE Exam Question

Read the following extract from Act 3 Scene 3 of 'Romeo and Juliet'. Answer the questions that follow.

At this point in the play, Romeo has just been banished from Verona and, in his despair, is trying to kill himself.

ROMEO:
Tell me, friar, tell me,
In what vile part of this anatomy
Doth my name lodge? Tell me, that I may sack
The hateful mansion.
Drawing his sword
FRIAR LAWRENCE:
Hold thy desperate hand:
Art thou a man? thy form cries out thou art:
Thy tears are womanish; thy wild acts denote
The unreasonable fury of a beast:
Unseemly woman in a seeming man!
Or ill-beseeming beast in seeming both!
Thou hast amazed me: by my holy order,
I thought thy disposition better temper'd.
Hast thou slain Tybalt? wilt thou slay thyself?
And stay thy lady too that lives in thee,
By doing damned hate upon thyself?

a) What do we learn about the Friar in this extract?
b) What do we learn about the Friar in the play as a whole?

 Sample GCSE Exam Answer

☑ Start with an overview

Friar Lawrence is the religious figure who acts as counsellor to the young lovers and whose plan ends in such tragedy. He is a central figure in the play yet whether we judge him as well-intentioned wise man or as an irresponsible meddler is open to interpretation.

☑ Start with the point that the Friar is an advisor/counsellor

In the extract, the Friar is presented as a counsellor as Romeo melodramatically asks him to advise him exactly where to stab himself. Romeo's **repetition** of the phrase **'tell me'** shows how he desperately seeks the Friar's help, establishing him to be a figure of importance in Romeo's life. This was demonstrated earlier in the play when Friar addresses Romeo as **'pupil mine'** and **'young son'**. The Friar is a teacher and the **possessive pronoun** 'mine' reflects his closeness to Romeo; later, the Friar and Romeo also share **rhyming couplets**, illustrating the bond between them. This bond is also captured in the words **'young son'**, and Romeo confides in the Friar when he cannot talk to his actual father. At this time, religious figures were often involved in the education of young noble children who would have a formal, distant relationship with their parents. In the extract, the Friar gives sensible advice, ordering Romeo to **'hold thy desperate hand!'** The **imperative verb** **'hold'** and the **exclamatory sentence** highlight his authority and urgency as he commands Romeo, who obeys.

The Friar is in a position of authority over Romeo, giving sound advice.

 Develop this point that the Friar is a person of authority

Not only is his authority like that as a parent, but his position as a religious figure means that he had a high status within the Elizabethan audience to whom Christianity was a fundamental part of their lives. We trust him as he has the authority of the Church behind him and his words **'by my holy order'** remind us of this authority. His role as spiritual advisor is also seen when he refers to Romeo's attempted suicide here as **'damned hate'**. Suicide was seen by the Elizabethans as a crime against God and the Friar's words reflect this attitude, warning Romeo that his proposed actions put him outside the Church's laws. His wisdom and goodness are clearly shown as he seeks to protect Romeo.

✓ Make the point that the Friar represents the theme of balancing opposing forces

This desire to protect is seen as the Friar scolds Romeo for extreme emotions and tells him to be more balanced and moderate, saying **'unseemly woman in a seeming man!... I thought thy disposition better temper'd.'** The language of opposites **'man' 'woman'** and **'unseemly' 'seeming'** reflects one of the themes of the play, that of conflict and clashes and the need to reconcile or balance opposing forces. We see this from the beginning, where the Friar is presented as a holy man who is linked to nature and who represents balance and harmony. When we first see him, the **setting** is **'outside'**, presumably in a garden, and the Friar is collecting herbs: **'baleful weeds/ precious-juiced flowers'**. Shakespeare creates a **semantic field** of opposing contrasts with **'day/night'** and **'weeds/flowers'** which highlights the theme of opposing forces that need to be balanced. The Friar seeks to be the one to balance these conflicting forces; the audience sees him as someone in touch with nature, collecting healing herbs and therefore he is viewed in a positive light, as a healer. His basket of herbs is also a **plot device**; the association with herbs early on means that the audience later implicitly (completely) believes the plot of the herbal potion giving Juliet the appearance of death.

✓ Develop the point that the Friar's role is that of a desire to bring peace to Verona

The Friar continues to play his role of being associated with peace and harmony by marrying the couple with positive words of union: **'Holy Church incorporate two in one'**. The blessing of the Church is given to the lovers and their relationship is within the safe boundaries of the Church. However, even this is not enough to ward off the evil fate that awaits them as the next scene is that of the hot, steamy afternoon in Verona when tempers run high and Mercutio and Tybalt are killed. This sharply **contrasts** with the peaceful wedding scene where the Friar plays his role of being associated with tranquillity and unity.

✓ Explore whether the Friar should be seen in a positive or negative light

This positive impression of Friar Lawrence is emphasised when he is described as a **'holy man'** by the Prince. This validation of his character by the most senior figure in the play guides our response to see him as a man with good intentions. His only motivation in the play is to reconcile the two warring families through the marriage of Romeo and Juliet; he says that he wishes to **'turn your households' rancour to pure love'**. This is a clear **statement** of intent, showing his deep and genuine desire to reconcile the opposite forces which have led to violence and conflict. However, he was fully aware of the possible outcomes of passionate love, even warning Romeo on his wedding day that **'violent delights have violent ends'**. His words here advise of the explosive nature of love; the **repetition** of the word **'violent'** issues a warning to the characters and to us, the audience. Therefore his actions were irresponsible, especially to an Elizabethan audience, who were very accustomed to marriages being made through parents, not secretly and without parental consent. In the Catholic society of 14th century Verona, the Friar has enormous power and he abuses this power. There is perhaps a sense that his belief in his own power allows him to play at God, giving Juliet the potion that will slow her heart and make her seem as dead; he is meddling with lives with disastrous consequences. Yet this power quickly ebbs away in the Capulets' tomb and he is quick to blame fate rather than take much responsibility for the events. A modern audience would probably be dismissive of this as a way of passing the blame, yet the Elizabethan audience would have firmly believed in predetermination, that our lives are set out for us by fate, and that the Friar was indeed helpless in the merciless workings of fate. Certainly, the character of the Friar and his role in the play remains open to interpretation.

Lord Capulet is a man of power in Verona whose feud with the Montagues plays a direct part in the death of his only daughter.

'Give me my long sword, ho!'

- His first words in Act 1 Scene 1 establish him as a commanding, hot-tempered man as he calls for his sword.

- The **imperative verb 'give'** shows how he is used to being obeyed, reflecting his status while the **interjection 'ho'** at the end illustrates his hasty temper.

- As head of a noble house, he would be in a position of authority. Yet he does not avoid violence but confronts it head-on, escalating the street brawl. His part in the tragic death of his child is established from the start.

Context: The nobility in 16th century England and 14th century Italy were often involved in political and personal feuds, vying for power; the Capulet/Montague feud would be a familiar scenario to the Elizabethan audience.

'hopeful lady of my earth'

- Capulet's language reflects his affection for Juliet; it gives her the respectful status of **'lady'** and the nature **metaphor** illustrates his deep paternal (fatherly) love for her.

- This courtly **image** shows his romanticised view of Juliet. However, later in the play, we question how well he knows his daughter; his view of her is perhaps idealistic rather than realistic.

'woo her, gentle Paris, get her heart'

- He adores Juliet and wants her to be happy, and puts off Paris' request for marriage based on her age. He wants her to be in a love match, although this is clearly forgotten later in the play when Juliet rejects Paris and his temper explodes.

Context: Girls were sometimes, but certainly not always, married at young ages in Elizabethan society but Capulet is unwilling to rush his own daughter's match. Thirteen is very young, even for the time period the play was set and written in.

'Does she not give us thanks?'

- The questions in Act 3 show Capulet's genuine confusion that Juliet has refused the match they have made for her with Paris. He is bewildered at her reaction as Juliet is not being an obedient daughter.

- He is also incredulous (surprised) that she is not grateful; he has fulfilled his parental duty in finding her a good match.

Context: Filial duty (filial refers to a son or daughter) meant that children in the 16th century were expected to completely obey their parents in all matters. Juliet's behaviour could have been seen as scandalous by the contemporary audience but, by allowing us to watch the blossoming of love between Romeo and Juliet, Shakespeare ensures that the audience is sympathetic to Juliet in this scene.

'Out you baggage! You tallow-face!'

- Capulet's hasty temper, as seen with his opening words in Act 1, explodes here as Juliet refuses to marry Paris. His fury is seen in the short, emphatic sentences while the range of insults used in this scene shows an unbalanced reaction to his daughter.

- **'Tallow'** relates to the animal fat in candle wax; he is definitely hurling deliberate insults at her. The *imperative verb* **'out'** illustrates the sense of commanding entitlement he has. Her disobedience reflects on his status.

- His vocabulary is vicious; **'baggage'** implies a woman of loose morals.

Context: In the 16th century, **'baggage'** would have been a vile insult to a girl from a noble household whose purity was a currency to be used in the marriage market.

| 'hang, beg, starve, die' | • The **violent verbs** he uses show the extent of his rage. The **monosyllabic** words are spat out in vicious fury. **Structurally**, this **foreshadows** the violence that will, in part at least, result from his fury; Juliet will indeed soon **'die'** as he suggests. |

• This reaction raises questions among the audience. Did he ever love Juliet if he can disown her so quickly? Is his love for her at the start bedded in a notion of a pretty, dutiful daughter rather than a real person?

• It could be that Capulet's reaction is so extreme because of the grief of losing his nephew, Tybalt. His reaction is completely unbalanced, and perhaps this is because he is in the throes of grief.

• There is a sharp **contrast** between his uncontrolled fury and Juliet's polite, calmer response to him as she calls him **'good father'**.

| 'our wedding cheer to a sad burial feast' | • Capulet's horrified distress is clear as he looks at his daughter's 'corpse' and realises that the day of celebration must now be one of mourning. |

• His language reflects the theme of **contrast** with **'wedding/burial, cheer/sad'**. Throughout the play, there is a theme of opposing forces that cause conflict and distress and this is seen in these lines.

Grade 9 Exploration:
Look at the ending in a different way

Does the ending show that Capulet and Montague have ended their feud?

Yes: Capulet promises to pay for a statue of Romeo that will match Montague's statue of Juliet, saying, **'as rich shall Romeo's by his lady's lie/Poor sacrifices of our enmity'**. **Structurally**, the Prologue's warning that the deaths will **'bury their parents' strife'** is now evident. The audience has watched the tragedy unfold until it concludes with Capulet's symbol of friendship and there is a sense of **resolution** in Capulet's acceptance that he and Montague have been to blame with their deadly **'enmity'** and that they need to make **'sacrifices'** to atone. The **rhyming couplet** of **'lie/enmity'** helps reaffirm the sense of **resolution** and show that Capulet has learnt lessons from the tragedy. The audience sees in Capulet a man who is ready to live in peace.

No: Capulet only mentions the statue of Romeo because Montague states how he intends to raise a statue of pure gold for Juliet first; this is an attempt to upstage Montague. Even at the end, in the midst of the death and grief, Capulet seems to be concerned about his status against the Montagues and not his daughter. It makes the audience wonder whether the feud is really settled and buried or whether there will be future conflict.

The *imperative verb* **'give'** shows how he is used to being obeyed, reflecting his status as head of a noble household.

Capulet's *metaphor* captures his deep paternal love for her. This *image* shows a romanticised view of Juliet and later on we question how well he knows her.

'Give me my long sword, ho!'

'hopeful lady of my earth'

Lord Capulet is shown as a man in command.

Capulet can be a loving father.

Lord Capulet

Capulet has a fierce temper which makes him a vicious father.

Does the ending show that Capulet and Montague have ended their feud?

'Hang, beg, starve, die'

Yes: 'As rich shall Romeo's by his lady's lie/Poor sacrifices of our enmity'. The play concludes with Capulet's symbol of friendship.

The violent *verbs* show the extent of his rage and *foreshadow* the violence that will, in part, result from his fury; Juliet will indeed **'die'.**

No: At the end, Capulet seems to be still concerned about his status against the Montagues and not his daughter.

Read the following extract from Act 3 Scene 5 of 'Romeo and Juliet'. Answer the questions that follow.

At this point in the play, Juliet has just refused to marry Paris.

CAPULET:
God's bread! it makes me mad:
Day, night, hour, tide, time, work, play,
Alone, in company, still my care hath been
To have her match'd: and having now provided
A gentleman of noble parentage,
Of fair demesnes, youthful, and nobly train'd,
Stuff'd, as they say, with honourable parts,
Proportion'd as one's thought would wish a man;
And then to have a wretched puling fool,
A whining mammet, in her fortune's tender,
To answer 'I'll not wed; I cannot love,
I am too young; I pray you, pardon me.'
But, as you will not wed, I'll pardon you:
Graze where you will you shall not house with me:
Look to't, think on't, I do not use to jest.
Thursday is near; lay hand on heart, advise:
An you be mine, I'll give you to my friend;
And you be not, hang, beg, starve, die in the streets,
For, by my soul, I'll ne'er acknowledge thee,
Nor what is mine shall never do thee good:
Trust to't, be think you; I'll not be forsworn.

a) What do we learn about Lord Capulet in this extract?

b) What do we learn about Lord Capulet in the play as a whole?

☑ Start with an overview

Lord Capulet is a man of power in Verona whose feud with the Montagues plays a direct part in the death of his only daughter. The audience witnesses his volatile temper fuel the conflict yet it is surely hard not to sympathise with his grief at the end when he finally understands the terrible consequences of hate and violence.

☑ Make the point that Lord Capulet has a quick temper

In this scene, Lord Capulet is furious, shown in the use of the blasphemous swearing of **'God's bread!'** The *exclamatory sentence* captures just how angry he is and this is clarified with the *declarative sentence* 'it makes me mad'; here, the *monosyllabic words* reflect the vicious force with which he is spitting out his rage. This hasty temper is also seen in his very first words in Act 1 when he shouts **'give me my long sword, ho'**, establishing him as a commanding, hot-tempered man. The *interjection* **'ho'** reveals his impatient nature while the *imperative verb* **'give'** shows how he is used to being obeyed, reflecting his status. As head of a noble house, he would be in a position of authority yet he does not avoid violence. Instead, he confronts it head-on, escalating the brawl and we see how the older generation fuels the feud that disrupts Verona and wonder how responsible the powerful Lord Capulet is. The nobility in 16th century England and 14th century Italy were often involved in political and personal feuds, vying for power; the Capulet/Montague feud would be a familiar scenario to the Elizabethan audience.

☑ Develop this point that Capulet is in a position of authority

Capulet's rage in the extract is a result of his daughter's defiance which he sees as a challenge to his authority. He states **'an you be mine, I'll give you to my friend'** and the **_possessive pronoun_** 'mine' reflects how he sees his daughter as a possession, to be handed over to his friend. The **_modal verb_** 'will' demonstrates how he has complete power over his daughter, and indeed, in 16th century England and 14th century Italy, girls were married at their parents' wishes, often to increase their parents' wealth or social/political position. The audience would have been accustomed to this patriarchal authority and would have understood his rage at being challenged.

☑ Make the point that Lord Capulet sees himself as a caring father

Capulet's rage is compounded because he views her defiance as unfounded. He states that **'my care hath been to have her match'd'**, seeing himself as a good father in arranging the match. However, the audience sees a cruel, abusive father as he uses insulting **_noun phrases_** such as **'wretched puling fool, a whining mammet'**. This reaction raises questions among the audience; did he ever love Juliet if he can disown her so quickly? Is his love for her at the start when he affectionately called her **'hopeful lady of my earth'** embedded in a notion of a pretty, dutiful daughter rather than a real person? Filial duty meant that children were expected to completely obey their parents in all matters and Juliet's behaviour in defying her father could have been seen as scandalous by the Elizabethan audience but, by allowing us to watch the blossoming of love between Romeo and Juliet throughout the play, Shakespeare ensures that the audience is sympathetic to Juliet in this scene, not to her father.

☑ Continue to examine Lord Capulet as a loving father

At the start of Act 1, we see a father who does seem to adore Juliet and wants her to be happy, putting off Paris' request for marriage based on her age as he says **'woo her, gentle Paris, get her heart'**. He wants her to be in a love match at this point, clearly desiring for her to be happy. Girls were sometimes, but certainly not always, married at young ages in Elizabethan society but Capulet is unwilling to rush his own daughter's match. Thirteen is very young, even for the time periods the play was set in and written in. Later, Capulet's horrified distress is clear as he looks at his dead daughter's corpse and realises that the day of celebration must now be one of mourning **'our wedding cheer to a sad burial feast'**. His language reflects the theme of contrast with **'wedding/burial, cheer/sad'**. Throughout the play, there is a theme of opposing forces that cause conflict and distress and this is seen in these lines.

☑ Explore the final impressions of Lord Capulet

At the end of the play, we see Capulet humbled and crushed through the tragic deaths of his daughter and her husband, promising to pay for a statue to remember the lovers: **'as rich shall Romeo's by his lady's lie/ Poor sacrifices of our enmity'**. **_Structurally_**, the Prologue's warning that the deaths will **'bury their parents' strife'** is now evident. The audience has watched the tragedy unfold until it concludes with Capulet's symbol of friendship and there is a sense of **_resolution_** in Capulet's acceptance that he and Montague have been to blame with their deadly **'enmity'** and that they need to make **'sacrifices'** to atone. The **_rhyming couplet_** of **'lie/ enmity'** helps reaffirm the sense of **_resolution_** and show that Capulet has learnt lessons from the tragedy. The audience sees in Capulet a man who is ready to live in peace. Yet there is an alternative way of viewing Lord Capulet at the end: not humbled at all but still seeking to maintain a position against the Montagues. Capulet only mentions the statue of Romeo because Montague states how he intends to raise a statue of pure gold for Juliet first; this is clearly an attempt to upstage the Montagues. It makes the audience wonder whether the feud is really settled and whether the impatient, autocratic Lord Capulet will really maintain the peace.

Prince Escalus is the absolute ruler of Verona and represents the public authority of the city.

'Three civil brawls... have thrice disturbed the quiet of our streets'

- Despite being the highest authority in Verona, the Prince is unable to contain the violence. **'Three'** times the feud has erupted; the **repetition** of **'three/thrice'** emphasises that this violence is out of control and may well erupt again.

- Shakespeare uses Prince Escalus' speech to establish an atmosphere of ongoing violence and hatred within the city of Verona. It is this atmosphere which will underpin the whole story and help shape events.

- Perhaps Shakespeare is showing, from the very beginning, that the Prince lacks control; the violence has already blown up three times. It is fate that controls the characters and sends Romeo and Juliet to their deaths, healing the rift between the households. Fate contrives (works) to bring about what Prince Escalus cannot- peace in Verona.

'Throw your mistempered weapons'

- The **imperative verb 'throw'** reflects the authority of the Prince. There is a **tone** of absolute authority here.

- His speech here is long and uninterrupted, demonstrating his status in the city.

Context: The Prince's absolute authority would have been familiar to the Elizabethan audience whose rulers had complete power over their subjects with minimal process of the law.

'Your lives shall pay the forfeit of the peace'

- The Prince's warning is a **plot device**. It is echoed by Romeo later in the play and adds dramatic tension as we know the stakes are high when Tybalt challenges Romeo in Act 3.

'cankered with peace to part your cankered hate'

- The Prince rebukes (tells off) the families for the fighting which has caused the elderly citizens of Verona to help stop the brawling.

- The Prince uses language of **contrast**. The opposition of **'peace'** and **'hate'** shows one of the themes of the play: conflicting ideas/ emotions that need to be resolved.

'I have an interest in your heart's proceedings'

- The Prince's decision to banish Romeo is influenced by his **'interest'** in the fight as Mercutio was his kinsman. He is not as impartial (unbiased) as he should be.

- There is perhaps a criticism here of the Prince and of rulers in general. They have absolute power but are not infallible (perfect).

'All are punished'

- At the end of the play, the Prince tells the assembled crowd and the audience that everyone has been hurt by the tragedy.

- This short emphatic **statement** rings very true and **contrasts** to some of his more formal, elaborate speeches which give him a pompous air. This line is heart-felt, and he includes himself in the punishment as he, too, has lost family members.

- Unlike Friar Lawrence, he accepts responsibility. He lays the blame for the tragedy on the people involved, including himself, not at fate's door, like Friar Lawrence does. With this sense of responsibility, there is a **resolution** at the close of the play.

Context: Shakespeare could be using Escalus as a model to the autocratic Queen Elizabeth, as a reminder that powerful leaders need to take responsibility for their people/cities/countries.

'The sun for sorrow will not show its head'

- The **personification** of the sun mourning the dead lovers highlights the scale of this tragedy. Even the cosmos (universe) is affected by the deaths of such young lovers. **Rhyming couplets** in this final speech help give the play a sense of **resolution** and conclusion.

Context: The Prince's words conclude the play; this fitted in with the literary convention of the time. It is significant that the final words are given to the most senior figure, acknowledging his authority and emphasising that his judgement, that this story is one of tragic woe, is correct.

Grade 9 Exploration:
Look at the character in a different way

Is the Prince just a symbol of authority?

Yes: The Prince's primary role in the play is that of the absolute ruler of Verona. He is used by Shakespeare to illustrate one of the main themes in the play: that of the individual versus society, the private life versus public life. Romeo and Juliet's private love is constantly affected by the public events, showing how hard it is for individual good to triumph over society's violence. The Prince is just the figurehead for this society and acts primarily as a *plot device*; his banishment of Romeo acts as the catalyst for the rest of the tragic events that follow.

No: The Prince displays a range of human characteristics which establish him as a character and not just a symbol of authority. He comes across as pompous in his opening speech with its formal *structure* and also as a man of violence, threatening his subjects with **'pain of torture'**. Later in the play, he shows weakness as a ruler when he admits to **'winking at your discords'** and shows real grief for the dead lovers in his *personification* of the sun refusing to show its head.

The answer to the question is best explored through the use of the *majestic plural pronoun* 'we' in Act 3. This reflects the sense of authority that the Prince holds, as 'we' includes not only the man but also God, the Law and the State. Elizabethan society believed in a rigid social structure with the monarch as central to society. Later in the speech, the Prince shifts to using the *personal pronoun* 'I' which shows how he has personally been affected by the death of his kinsman, Mercutio; **'I have an interest in your hate's proceedings'**. The shift in *pronoun* reflects one of the themes of the play, that of the individual versus society. Shakespeare shows us how conflict is created when individual desires or needs do not coincide with society's needs.

Essential Exam Tips

☑ Look for strong words/phrases/images in the extract and try to write about the effect these have.

☑ Keep an eye on the time. Write the time that you need to have finished this Shakespeare question on a piece of paper and stick to it.

The *imperative verb* 'throw' shows the complete power of the Prince. Elizabethan audiences would have been used to rulers with absolute authority.

Repetition of **'three/thrice'** emphasises that this violence is out of control and may well erupt again.

Shakespeare is establishing an atmosphere of ongoing violence.

'Throw your mistempered weapons'

'Three civil brawls... have thrice disturbed the quiet of our streets'

The Prince is absolute ruler in Verona.

The Prince is not an effective ruler.

The Prince

The Prince ends the play; the literary convention of the time gave the last words to the most senior figure.

Is the Prince just a symbol of authority?

'The sun for sorrow will not show its head'

Yes: **'we do exile him'**. The use of the *majestic plural pronoun* **'we'** shows that the Prince represents the Law and the State; he is just a figurehead.

The *personification* of the sun mourning the dead lovers highlights the scale of this tragedy and we agree with the Prince's judgement that this is a story of woe.

No: The Prince moves to a *personal pronoun*: **'I have an interest'**. This shows him as an individual who is emotionally affected by events.

Read the following extract from Act 3 Scene 1 of 'Romeo and Juliet'.

Answer both questions below the text.

At this point in the play, the Prince is dealing with the aftermath of the deaths of Mercutio and Tybalt.

PRINCE:
And for that offence
Immediately we do exile him hence:
I have an interest in your hate's proceeding,
My blood for your rude brawls doth lie a-bleeding;
But I'll amerce you with so strong a fine
That you shall all repent the loss of mine:
I will be deaf to pleading and excuses;
Nor tears nor prayers shall purchase out abuses:
Therefore use none: let Romeo hence in haste,
Else, when he's found, that hour is his last.
Bear hence this body and attend our will:
Mercy but murders, pardoning those that kill.

a) Discuss how the Prince is presented in this extract.

b) Discuss how the Prince is presented in the play as a whole.

Sample GCSE Exam Answer

 Start with an overview

Prince Escalus is the absolute ruler of Verona and represents the public authority of the city and, in this extract, his power is evident as he banishes Romeo from the city-state. He only appears on stage three times in the play yet his role in the tragedy is an interesting one to explore .

 Make the point that the Prince is in a position of absolute authority in Verona

The Prince passes summary judgement on Romeo, declaring **'immediately we do exile him hence'**. The use of the **adverb 'immediately'** at the start of the line places emphasis at how swiftly he has sentenced Romeo, based on the testimony of just one person, Benvolio. We see him make instant, possibly too hasty decisions, yet the Prince's absolute authority would have been familiar to the Elizabethan audience whose rulers had complete power over their subjects with minimal process of the law. The use of the **majestic plural pronoun 'we'** reflects again the sense of authority that the Prince holds, as **'we'** suggests he is speaking both as an individual and as someone who represents the law and the state. The formal sentence construction **'we do exile'** works to continue to evoke (create) a sense of weighty authority.

 Move to the point that the Prince is also an individual who has been affected by events

In the rest of the speech, the Prince shifts to using the **personal pronoun 'I'** which reflects how he has personally been affected by the death of his kinsman, Mercutio; **'I have an interest in your hate's proceedings'**. The shift in **pronoun** reflects one of the themes of the play: that of the individual versus society.

Shakespeare shows us how conflict is created when individual desires and needs do not coincide with society's needs. The Prince is not the impartial (unbiased) ruler he should be; he is influenced by the murder of his kinsman, and, by banishing Romeo, the Prince sets in motion the tragic events that will follow. It is his anger that motivates him, as can be seen in the line **'my blood for your rude brawls lie a-bleeding'**, his rage evident in the **monosyllables** and the **plosive** 'b's.

☑ Move to the point that the Prince is presented as a strong man

The Prince proves himself to be a strong man through the use of **imperative verbs** **'let' 'bear' 'attend'** which reflect his sense of power. He is also implacable (not easy to persuade) as he makes the definite **statement** **'I will be deaf to pleadings and excuses'**; once he has declared the punishment, the **modal verb** **'will'** shows that he is not going to change his mind. This sense of finality from a man who has made up his mind is also seen in the **rhyming couplets** which create an impression of gravitas and decisiveness.

☑ Continue to explore whether the Prince is a strong ruler after all

Yet, despite being the highest authority in Verona, the Prince is unable to contain the violence. In Act 1 scene 1, the Prince states that **'three civil brawls… have thrice disturbed the quiet of our streets'**. The **repetition** of **'three/thrice'** emphasises that this violence is out of control and may well erupt again. Shakespeare uses Prince Escalus' speech to establish an atmosphere of ongoing violence and hatred within the city of Verona. It is this atmosphere which will underpin the whole story and help shape events. Perhaps Shakespeare is showing, from the very beginning, that the Prince lacks control; the violence has already blown up three times. It is fate that controls the characters and sends Romeo and Juliet to their deaths, healing the rift between the households. Fate contrives (works) to bring about what Prince Escalus cannot: peace in Verona.

☑ Explore how the Prince voices the moral of the story: that violence leads to suffering for all

Shakespeare follows the five act **structure** of tragedy used by the ancient Greeks; the final act is the **resolution** where lessons are learned by the tragedy. At the end of the play, the Prince tells the assembled crowd and the audience that everyone has been hurt by the tragedy: **'all are punished.'** This short emphatic **statement** rings very true and **contrasts** to some of his more formal, elaborate speeches which give him a pompous air. This line is genuine, heart-felt, and he includes himself in the punishment as he has, too, lost family members. He lays the blame for the deaths on the people involved, not at fate's door, like Friar Lawrence does. There is a sense of responsibility and, in that, there is a **resolution** at the close of the play. It is possible that Shakespeare is subtly showing that rulers should take responsibility for their own actions. If Escalus had been more effectual as a ruler- less autocratic, perhaps- then the feud might have been resolved without the deaths of the young lovers. The **personification** of the sun mourning the dead lovers highlights the scale of this tragedy. Even the cosmos (universe) is affected by the deaths of such young lovers. **Rhyming couplets** in this final speech help give the play this important sense of **resolution**. The Prince's words conclude the play; this fitted in with the literary convention of the time. It is significant that the final words are given to the most senior figure, acknowledging his authority and emphasising that his judgement, that this story is one of tragic woe, is correct.

Mercutio is a vibrant, memorable character who serves as a **contrast** to Romeo's view of romantic love and is also used as a **plot device**.

'that dreamers often lie'

- When Romeo speaks of his love for Rosaline and how he has dreamed of her, Mercutio dismisses this with the pithy (short) **statement** 'that dreamers often lie'.

- This brisk **statement** presents Mercutio as a good friend, one who will try to shake Romeo out of his misery. It also perhaps shows that, despite being friends, they are very different characters. It is interesting that Romeo does not confide in Mercutio in the hours that follow.

- Mercutio's quick retort (response) also illustrates his sharp intelligence.

- His words dismiss dreams and portents (dreams that predict the future) as nonsense. Yet we remember this cynicism later when Mercutio curses the two households with such devastating consequences.

- Mercutio goes on to paint a vivid world of dreams in his Queen Mab speech. This long colourful speech builds tension as the men head to the Capulets' party.

'Queen Mab... with blisters plagues...'

- Mercutio describes Queen Mab, the bringer of dreams.

- His view of love refers to the physical side, that of sexual intercourse. His speech is full of unpleasant **images** such as disease **'with blisters plagues'**, a reference to sexually transmitted diseases. **'Plagues'** and **'blisters'** are words that are associated with pain and danger.

- Shakespeare uses Mercutio to show a different side to love, reminding us that love is complex and varied, and that the perfect view of love illustrated by Romeo and Juliet has another, less pleasant side.

Context: The references to sexually transitted diseases and the pain they bring would have been recognisable and relevant to the Elizabethan audience, where STDs such as syphilis were rife and medical remedies were almost non-existent.

• Mercutio's role is also that of a comic character. Here he is teasing Romeo about love, using sexual innuendo as he refers to a fruit that looks like genitalia. The actor playing Mercutio would certainly be using his body and facial expressions to make the most of the comic lines.

• Similarly, the **long vowel sounds** of **'open arse'** and the short, jaunty (cheerful) **alliteration** of the 'p' in **'pop'rin pear'** lend themselves to comic acting and the amusement of the audience.

• In Act 3, Mercutio cannot understand Romeo's refusal to fight with Tybalt.

• His language reflects his disgust at Romeo's peace-keeping and the **triplet** of **adjectives** **'calm dishonourable vile'** shows his growing anger which soon explodes, adding to the tension of this scene.

• Shakespeare relies heavily on **dramatic irony** in this scene. The audience has knowledge that Mercutio does not; Romeo is not fighting because he has just married Juliet, Tybalt's cousin. Shakespeare uses this **dramatic irony** to create tension; we understand the characters' emotions and actions but they react to each other without the knowledge that the audience has. It makes the deaths of Mercutio and Tybalt more dramatic and more painful because we, the audience, fully understand how unnecessary these deaths are.

Context: **Masculine honour was viewed as very important in Elizabethan society. Shakespeare's audience would understand Mercutio's outrage at allowing an insult to go undefended.**

• The use of a **pun** highlights Mercutio's wit, even as he dies. The humour here (**'grave'** means serious and also means being buried when he is dead) illustrates his bright intelligence and sense of wit; his mind is able to use **wordplay**, which the Elizabethan audience loved, even as his body fails him.

• Shakespeare uses him as a tool for **comic relief** in the play; his comic **puns** and insults in Act 3 Scene 1 remind us that he is a light-hearted, likeable character, which only serves to highlight the tragedy of his death.

- Mercutio's final words curse both the Montagues and Capulets.

- **Structurally**, the curse is shown to be immediately effective as Romeo murders Tybalt and is banished, leading to the fatal end of the play.

- Shakespeare does this to remind us of the relentless power of fate and how its path is consistently followed by the characters.

- Mercutio's death marks a turning point in the play; the play loses all comic elements from then on.

Grade 9 Exploration:
Look at the character in a different way

Is Mercutio part of fate's plan?

Yes: His last words place the emphasis on fate as he curses both the Montagues and Capulets who will soon lose their precious children. He blames the feud between the households as the cause of his death.

No: His own hot temper causes the fatal fight; from the very beginning of Act 3, he escalates the violence as he says **'make it a word and a blow'**; the threat of physical violence and the challenge in the **imperative verb** **'make'** ramps up the sense of antagonism and tension. Shakespeare is, perhaps, suggesting that our actions shape our fate; if Mercutio had a different temperament, then the vicious violence of this scene could have been avoided.

Elizabethans held firm views on predetermination, believing that our lives are mapped out for us by fate, which could be kind or cruel. Shakespeare was interested in self-determination, that our own actions influence fate and have clear consequences.

Essential Exam Tips

☑ Aim for five detailed paragraphs; your response will be evaluated on quality not quantity but it's difficult to make your response good if it is brief or lacking in detail.

☑ Most of the exam boards require you to write about context. Check whether your exam board gives marks for this and, if it does, make sure you weave points about Shakespeare's audience and the literary conventions that Shakespeare uses into your response.

The negative **vocabulary** refers to sexually transmitted disease, **contrasting** with Romeo's idealised view of love.

This **pun** on the word **'grave'** reminds the audience that he is a lively, witty character and so emphasises the tragedy and violence of his death.

'Queen Mab... with blisters plagues'

'Ask for me tomorrow and you shall find me a grave man'

Mercutio is used as a *foil* (contrast) to Romeo as he talks of the physical side of love.

Shakespeare uses Mercutio as a comic character to amuse the audience.

Mercutio

Mercutio is an honourable, loyal friend.

Is Mercutio part of fate's plan?

'O calm dishonourable vile submission'

Yes: 'A plague o' both your houses!' The **repetitive** phrase emphasises the curse which he places on the families. We immediately see the consequences of this curse as Romeo is banished.

Masculine honour was viewed as very important in Elizabethan society. The audience would understand Mercutio's outrage at allowing an insult to go undefended.

No: His own hot temper leads him into the fight: **'make it a word and a blow'**. His own actions, not fate, lead to tragedy.

Sample GCSE Exam Question

Read the following extract from Act 3 Scene 1 of 'Romeo and Juliet'.

Answer both questions below the text.

At this point in the play, Mercutio has been fatally wounded by Tybalt.

MERCUTIO:
No, 'tis not so deep as a well, nor so wide as a
church-door; but 'tis enough,' twill serve: ask for
me to-morrow, and you shall find me a grave man. I am peppered, I warrant, for this world. A plague o'
both your houses! 'Zounds, a dog, a rat, a mouse, a
cat, to scratch a man to death! a braggart, a
rogue, a villain, that fights by the book of
arithmetic! Why the devil came you between us? I
was hurt under your arm.

ROMEO:
I thought all for the best.

MERCUTIO:
Help me into some house, Benvolio,
Or I shall faint. A plague o' both your houses!
They have made worms' meat of me: I have it,
And soundly too: your houses!

a) How is Mercutio is presented in this extract?

b) How is Mercutio is presented in the play as a whole?

Sample GCSE Answer

 ☑ Start with an overview

Mercutio is a vibrant, memorable character whose witty banter endears him to audiences and whose bawdy attitude towards love serves as a ***contrast*** to Romeo's romantic view. In the extract, Mercutio's role as a ***plot device*** is evident as he curses the feuding families that have caused his death and sets in motion the events that lead to the tragic end of the play.

☑ Make the point that Mercutio is used by Shakespeare as a comic character

The use of a ***pun*** on the word **'grave'** shows Mercutio's wit, even as he dies. The humour here (**'grave'** means serious and also means being buried as he will be dead) illustrates his bright intelligence and sense of wit; his mind is able to use ***wordplay*** even as his body fails him. There is a real sense of tragedy that someone so witty and vibrant is dying and the black humour, spoken in ***prose*** as opposed to ***blank verse***, works as a ***contrast*** to the violence and drama in the scene. Shakespeare uses him as a tool for ***comic relief*** elsewhere in the play with his bawdy jokes to amuse his audience, who would have been fidgeting and chatting; humour would have been a device to hold their attention. An example is when he teases Romeo about love, shouting **'she were an open arse, thou a pop'rin pear'**, and using sexual innuendo as he refers to a fruit that looks like genitalia. The actor playing Mercutio would also certainly be using his body and facial expressions to make the most of the comic lines. The long **vowel sounds** of **'open arse'** and the short, jaunty (cheerful) **alliteration** of the 'p' in **'pop'rin pear'** lend themselves to comic acting and amusement.

✓ Make the point that Mercutio is shown as an honourable man

Mercutio instructs Benvolio to **'help me into some house, Benvolio, Or I shall faint'**, showing his reluctance to reveal his weakness in front of others. There is urgency in the **imperative verb** **'help'** but Mercutio continues to joke as he goes. In Elizabethan society, masculine honour was linked to bravery so it is a matter of honour that he dies a 'man's death' without showing weakness. This sense of honour is also shown when he sees Romeo's refusal to fight as **'calm dishonourable vile submission'**. His language reflects his disgust at Romeo's peace-keeping and the **triplet** of **adjectives** reflects his growing anger which soon explodes, adding to the tension of this scene.

✓ Make the point that Mercutio is used as a *plot device* to show the change in events

Mercutio's final words **'plague o' both your houses!'** are **repeated** for maximum impact as he curses both the Montagues and Capulets. **Structurally**, the curse is shown to be immediately effective as Romeo murders Tybalt and is banished, leading to the fatal end of the play. Shakespeare does this to remind us of the relentless power of fate and how its path is consistently followed by the characters. Mercutio's death serves as a turning point in the play; events that follow his death accelerate towards the final suicides. It marks the end of the comic elements of the play and the play moves to full tragedy.

✓ Explore whether Mercutio is part of fate's plan

Shakespeare uses Mercutio to explore ideas about fate and self-determination. Elizabethans held firm views on predetermination, believing that our lives are mapped out for us by a fate which can be kind or cruel. Mercutio's last words reflect this emphasis on the power of fate as he curses both the Montagues and Capulets; this curse is soon seen to work as both households lose their precious children. He blames the feud between the households as the cause of his death. Yet surely Mercutio himself is to blame for his own death. His own hot temper causes the fatal fight; from the very beginning of Act 3, he escalates the violence as he taunts Tybalt with **'make it a word and a blow'**. The threat of physical violence and the challenge in the **imperative verb** **'make'** ramps up the sense of aggression and tension. Shakespeare is, perhaps, suggesting that our actions shape our fate; if Mercutio had a different temperament then the vicious violence of this scene could have been avoided. Shakespeare was interested in self-determination, that our own actions influence our fate and have consequences; he uses Mercutio to explore this idea.

✓ Make the point that Mercutio is used as a *foil* (contrast) to Romeo

Shakespeare also uses Mercutio to explore different aspects to the concept of love. While Romeo holds love and women to be pure and untouchable, Mercutio shows the audience the other side to love. He describes Queen Mab, the bringer of dreams, using words that are associated with pain and disease such as **'plagues'** and **'blisters'**, a reference to sexually transmitted diseases, the likely consequence of sexual intercourse. These references would have been recognisable and relevant to the Elizabethan audience, where STDs such as syphilis were rife and medical remedies were almost non-existent. Shakespeare uses Mercutio as a **foil** to Romeo and shows a different side to love, reminding us that love is complex and varied, and that the perfect view of love illustrated by Romeo and Juliet has another, less pleasant side. His **vocabulary** provides a dark edge that would unsettle the audience and create a sense of unease. Overall, Mercutio is a complex, likeable character whose death is a needless tragedy that highlights the senseless, brutal violence running through Verona.

Tybalt of the Capulet family and Benvolio from the Montague household serve as *foils* (opposites) to each other; one is hot-tempered and violent while the other is a peacemaker. Shakespeare uses them as opposites to highlight the ideas of violence and peace in the play.

'I do but keep the peace'

- In the opening scene, Benvolio is trying to stop the servants from fighting. As Tybalt enters, Benvolio attempts to prevent the situation from escalating.

- Benvolio's clear emphatic **statement** establishes him as a peacemaker.

- It also shows him as brave, refusing to give in to Tybalt's desire for bloodshed.

- His words **contrast** with Tybalt's words (see below), highlighting the theme of opposing contradictions which need to be reconciled (brought together) in order for the violence to end.

'Peace? I hate the word, as I hate hell, all Montagues and thee'

- Tybalt responds to Benvolio's desire to keep the peace. The use of the question **'peace?'** shows how Tybalt has no understanding of the word. He is so violent that he rejects all ideas of peace.

Context: To an Elizabethan audience, with the Christian attitude to hell being one of pain and horror, this was a particularly potent (strong) *image*.

- The **repetition** of the **verb 'hate'** shows Tybalt's angry nature and the short, **monosyllabic statement** makes it clear how passionately he is linked to violence and how he is infected with the hatred that dominates the play.

- Tybalt's words connect hell and the Montagues, associating the Montagues with the devil. This is an irrational and corrosive hatred, demonstrating just how lost in the feud the Capulet and Montagues are that their kinsmen use such dramatic **vocabulary**.

'I weep… at thy good heart's oppression'	• Benvolio shows compassion for Romeo's sadness over Rosaline. His kindness helps establish his character as a positive force for good in Verona.

'I'll not endure him' / 'He shall be endured'	• Tybalt is furious at Romeo's intrusion into the Capulet ball and says that **'I'll not endure him'**, seeking to remove him by violence. His uncle, Lord Capulet, tells him to back down, saying **'he shall be endured'**. • Tybalt's use of the ***modal verb*** **'will'** shows his clear commitment to the violence he intends. His fury is evident at the slight to his family honour as he sees it as a deadly insult that Romeo has dared come to the Capulets' house. He seems to lack self-control in that he cannot suppress his anger. • However, Lord Capulet exerts his authority, forcibly telling him that Romeo must be allowed to stay unmolested. Lord Capulet chastises (tells off) Tybalt, calling him **'saucy'** and belittling him. Tybalt is humiliated which surely only increases his determination to avenge himself on Romeo.	Context: **Tybalt's initial defiance of his uncle would have been disapproved of by contemporary audiences. Capulet is head of the household and Tybalt, as the young nephew, should have given him the respect that Elizabethans would have regarded as his due.**

'The day is hot, the Capulets are abroad' 	• In Act 3, Benvolio, the peacemaker, gives us clear warning that trouble is coming. ***Foreshadowing*** is used so that when the Capulets appear, the audience is tensely waiting in anticipation for the fight that will follow. His words are prophetic; they do indeed meet the Capulets and become involved in a deadly fight. • ***Pathetic fallacy*** is clear in these words; the **'hot'** sun reflects the hot tempers that will soon explode.	Context: **Shakespeare's theatre was limited in terms of special effects so Benvolio's words also work to tell the audience the time of day.**

'Boy, this shall not excuse the injuries'	• Tybalt holds onto his grudge despite Romeo's polite response to his own insult. • He calls Romeo **'boy'** which is insulting. His words show how he is refusing to compromise; he is definitely looking for a fight.	Context: **Masculine honour was viewed as very important in Elizabethan society; Shakespeare's audience would understand Tybalt's outrage at allowing an insult to go undefended.**
'stout Mercutio... stout Tybalt'	• Benvolio gives a fair account of the fight to the Prince. • The *adjective* of **'stout'** is given to both Montague and Capulet, showing that Benvolio is unbiased in his telling of the story. • He is seen as trustworthy; his name means 'good-will'.	

Grade 9 Exploration:
Look at the character in a different way

Is Tybalt the villain of the play?

Yes: He searches out Romeo, deliberately seeking out violence and he kills Mercutio **'under Romeo's arm'**. This was foul play (cheating) with nothing honorable about it. He is the embodiment of the violence and hate that act to destroy the pure love of Romeo and Juliet; Shakespeare purposefully adds the fight scene in Act 1 which was not in the original 1562 story by Brooke. This establishes Tybalt from the opening as an incredibly violent, dangerous character.

No: Tybalt is not the archetypal villain such as Iago in 'Othello' whose motive is pure malice. His noble birth means that he has a finely tuned sense of status and his challenge of Romeo follows a code of honour; this is seen with his initally courteous and formal greeting of the Montagues in Act 3 as he says **'gentlemen, good den'**. He is motivated by honour not violence, and indeed, it could be argued that he is a product of the violence of Verona, not a cause of the violence (see context below).

Elizabethan society, and that of Verona in the fourteenth century, was a much more violent one than we experience. Tybalt would have been trained from a young age to fight and would not have been expected to work. Without a job, Tybalt would have been without an occupation; much of his aggression is perhaps down to the fact that he is just a young man wandering around looking for trouble.

The clear *statement* of intent illustrates his determination to stop the violence.

The use of the question **'peace?'** shows how Tybalt has no understanding of the word. He is so violent that he rejects all ideas of peace.

'I do but keep the peace'

'Peace? I hate the word'

Benvolio is a peacemaker.

Tybalt is a violent character.

Benvolio & Tybalt

Benvolio and Tybalt act as opposites in the play.

Is Tybalt the villain of the play?

'Peace? I hate the word'

Yes: He is the embodiment of violence and hate that act to destroy the pure love of Romeo and Juliet.

Benvolio and Tybalt reflect one of the themes of the play: that of contradictions which need to be reconciled (brought together) in order for the violence to end.

No: He is a product of the violence of Verona and only seeks to uphold family honour.

Sample GCSE Exam Question

Read the following extract from Act 3 Scene 1 of 'Romeo and Juliet'.

Answer both questions below the text.

At this point in the play, Tybalt is looking for Romeo in order to avenge the 'insult' of Romeo attending the Capulets' party.

BENVOLIO:
We talk here in the public haunt of men:
Either withdraw unto some private place,
And reason coldly of your grievances,
Or else depart; here all eyes gaze on us.

MERCUTIO:
Men's eyes were made to look, and let them gaze;
I will not budge for no man's pleasure, I.
Enter ROMEO

TYBALT:
Well, peace be with you, sir: here comes my man.

MERCUTIO:
But I'll be hanged, sir, if he wear your livery:
Marry, go before to field, he'll be your follower;
Your worship in that sense may call him 'man.'

TYBALT:
Romeo, the hate I bear thee can afford
No better term than this,--thou art a villain.

a) Discuss how Tybalt and Benvolio are presented in this extract.

b) Discuss how Tybalt and Benvolio are presented in the play as a whole.

Sample GCSE Answer

 Start with an overview

Tybalt of the Capulet family and Benvolio from the Montague household serve as **_foils_** (opposites) to each other; one is hot-tempered and violent while the other is a peacemaker. Shakespeare uses them as opposites to highlight the idea of contradictions that clash and so need to be resolved.

 Make the point that Benvolio is established as a peacekeeper

In the extract, the audience sees the men's different natures and attitudes. Benvolio is keen to defuse the situation, telling the other men to **'reason coldly of your grievances'**. The **_adverb_ 'coldly'** is the opposite to the **'hot'** day that leads to hot tempers that Benvolio has already uneasily commentated on. This reflects one of the themes of the play: the theme of opposing contradictions which need to be reconciled in order for the violence to end. This ideas of opposites is also seen in the clash between **'public haunt'** and **'private space'**. Benvolio is used to remind us of the conflict that follows individuals who seek personal justice in defiance of public rulings.

Develop this point about conflict between opposites

This theme of the clash of opposites is shown through the characters of Tybalt and Benvolio themselves. While Benvolio advises discussion rather than violence, Tybalt is actively confrontational. In Act 1, he proved himself as the embodiment of the vicious feud which dominates Verona when he says, incredulously, **'peace? I hate the word, as I hate hell, all Montagues and thee'**. The use of the question in **'peace?'** shows that he has no comprehension of this word, so infected is he with violence, and the linking of the Montagues to hell reveals his irrational hatred that the original, deeply Christian audience would have seen as disturbing. In the extract, this antagonic attitude is seen as he deliberately insults Romeo, stating that **'thou art a villain'**. This was a real insult in the strict social ordering of Elizabethan society when **'villain'** implied someone of low-class.

Make the point that Tybalt is motivated by family honour

Tybalt could be seen to have good reason for his anger against Romeo as he is furious at the perceived slight to the Capulets' honour when Romeo intruded into their party. Elizabethan society was defined by a strong sense of family loyalty and honour and Tybalt reflects this attitude when he tells his uncle **'I'll not endure him'**. His use of the **modal verb 'will'** reflects his clear commitment to the violence he intends and also shows a lack of self-control in that he cannot suppress his anger. However, Lord Capulet exerts his authority, forcibly telling him that Romeo must be allowed to stay unmolested. Lord Capulet chastises (tells off) Tybalt, calling him **'saucy'** and belittling him. Tybalt is humiliated which surely only increases his determination to avenge himself on Romeo.

Examine Benvolio's role as a symbol for good

Shakespeare uses Benvolio partly as a **symbol** of peace and partly as a **plot device**. He is first seen trying to prevent violence in Act 1, stating **'I do but keep the peace'**. His clear emphatic **statement** of intent reveals him to be a man of peace. Certainly, his very name means 'good-will', reflecting his purpose as peace-maker. This is further shown in his fair, impartial account of the fight when he uses the **adjective 'stout'** to describe both Mercutio and Tybalt. He also helps move the plot along by urging Romeo to attend the Capulets' party, and his words at the start of Act 3, commenting that **'the day is hot, the Capulets are abroad'** create dramatic tension for the audience as his words **foreshadow** the violence that follows. Yet Benvolio is also a character in his own right; he comes across as humorous when he joins in the male banter and he is seen as a loyal friend when he attempts to help Romeo overcome his misery over Rosaline, showing great compassion with his kind words of **'I weep... at thy good heart's oppression'**.

Explore whether Tybalt is the villain of the play

Tybalt is the most aggressive character in the play. He searches out Romeo, deliberately seeking out violence and he kills Mercutio **'under Romeo's arm'**. This was foul play (cheating) with nothing honorable about it. He is the embodiment of the violence and hate that act to destroy the pure love of Romeo and Juliet; interestingly, Shakespeare deliberately adds the fight scene in Act 1 which was not in the original 1562 story by Brooke. This establishes Tybalt from the opening as an incredibly violent, dangerous character. Yet we should question this interpretation and ask ourselves if Tybalt deserves to be villified; Tybalt is not the archetypal villain such as Iago in 'Othello' whose motive is pure malice. His noble birth means that he has a finely tuned sense of status and his challenge of Romeo follows a code of honour with his initally courteous greeting of the Montagues of **'gentlemen, good den'**. Indeed, in the extract, he turns away from Mercutio, saying **'peace be with you, sir'**, showing that he does have self-control. He is motivated by honour not violence, and indeed, it could be argued that he is a product of the violence of Verona, not a cause of the violence. Elizabethan society, and that of Verona in the fourteenth century, was a much more violent one than the one we live in. Tybalt would have been trained from a young age to fight and would not have been expected to work. Without a job, Tybalt would have been without an occupation; how much is his aggression down to the fact that he is just a bored young man wandering around looking for trouble? Benvolio and Tybalt are certainly **symbols** of peace and violence in a play about the clashing of opposite forces yet they are also interesting characters that enrich the play.

Love is at the centre of the play and drives much of the action. Shakespeare uses the characters to explore the many different aspects of love.

'O she doth teach the torches to burn bright!'

- Love is seen as an overwhelming and positive emotion.
- The **metaphor** is a spontaneous outburst of passion which is full of emotion; the **plosive 'b'** sounds capture Romeo's passion and enthusiasm.
- The **metaphor** also associates Juliet with light, a positive **image** showing her to be dazzling. Light is a **symbol** of hope which conveys to us that love is a force for good in the violence of Verona.

'make blessed my rude hand'

- Romeo sees himself as profane (not religious) but improves himself and blesses himself when he touches Juliet's hand upon first meeting her. This reflects the conflict between the profane and the sacred in the play.
- Juliet is constantly seen as pure and sacred with religious **imagery** such as **'bright angel'** used to describe her. Romeo is seen as more down-to-earth. This is reflected in the staging of the balcony scene when Juliet is above Romeo.
- The conflict between the profane and the secular is reconciled when Romeo and Juliet are married and so have the blessing of the Church. Love is presented as a pure and elevating emotion which improves Romeo.

Context: The religious *imagery* validates the pure nature of Romeo and Juliet's love so that when the couple commit suicide, seen as a serious sin by the Church, the contemporary, Christian audience still feels sympathy.

- Nurse uses **puns**, making crude sexual reference to Juliet's wedding night.

- Shakespeare uses the Nurse as a **contrast** to the purity of the young lovers' feelings for each other, revealing the physical side to love.

Context: Shakespeare's original audience would have enjoyed the play on words and the bawdy humour. In the theatre, the audience would have been standing in front of the stage, fidgeting and chatting, so humour would have been a device to hold their attention.

'too rash, too unadvised, too sudden'

- Juliet is aware of the possible consequences of their love, and the anxiety captured in this **tri-colon** here reminds Romeo, and the audience, of the many negatives to their love. It is not just foolish, but it is rushed; the **tri-colon** emphasises that this love is not straightforward and could, and indeed will, be dangerous.

'Spread thy close curtain, love-performing night'

- Love is seen as a force that changes the characters. Juliet is impatient for night-time as she waits for her husband on their wedding night and the **imperative verb** 'spread' portrays Juliet here as passionate and hot-blooded, full of desire for her new husband. We see her development from the beginning of the play when, shy and demure, she waited on her parents' pleasure. Here, she is seeking her own pleasure and the **command verbs** capture this control she has taken over her own life.

- Juliet's sexuality and the physical pleasures of love are clearly shown here, safely shown, as she is now married.

Context: Sex outside marriage would be outside the boundaries of acceptable behaviour in the Elizabethan era; as she is now legally married in a holy ceremony, Shakespeare can show Juliet's sexual side.

> **'These violent delights have violent ends'**

- Love and violence are seen as two sides of the same coin. Even the lovers' wedding day is underscored with references to death. Friar Lawrence's words here warn of the explosive nature of love; the **repetition** of the word **'violent'** issues a warning to the characters and to us.

- One of the themes of the play is that of conflict and clashes and the need to reconcile opposing forces; love and violent hatred are in direct opposition throughout the play and are only reconciled at the end.

Grade 9 Exploration:
Look at the theme in a different way

Does love triumph over violence?

Yes: Although the play ends with their tragic suicides, Romeo and Juliet's love has ensured peace and harmony in Verona. Capulet promises to pay for a statue of Romeo that will match Montague's statue of Juliet, saying **'as rich shall Romeo's by his lady's lie/Poor sacrifices of our enmity'**. **Structurally**, the Prologue's warning or promise that the deaths will **'bury their parents' strife'** is now evident. Shakespeare uses the classic five act **structure** of Greek tragedy in order to end with a **resolution**; with Capulet's symbol of friendship, the audience feels a sense of **catharsis** and closure and this is emphasised with the use of **rhyming couplets 'lie/enmity'**. Love has ensured that the violence in Verona is over.

No: Capulet only mentions the statue of Romeo because Montague states how he intends to raise a statue of pure gold for Juliet first; this is a clear attempt to upstage his old foe. Even at the end, in the midst of the death and grief, Capulet seems to be concerned about his status against the Montagues and not his daughter. It makes the audience wonder whether the feud is really settled and buried or whether there will be future conflict; it seems that the love of Romeo and Juliet will be forgotten and nothing will have been learnt.

Essential Exam Tips

☑ When writing about themes, make sure you explain how the ideas affect the characters and also apply to the audience.

☑ Exam boards use different wording for the Shakespeare question. Check with your teacher or the exam board's website to see if you have to answer part a) and part b) separately OR whether you can weave the questions on the extract and the whole play together into one answer.

The *imperative verb* 'spread' shows Juliet's impatience for her wedding night. Love has changed her from the shy, compliant girl at the start.

This bawdy (rude) **pun** about sex on Juliet's wedding night **contrasts** with the pure romantic love of Romeo and Juliet.

'Spread thy close curtain, love-performing night'

'You shall bear the burden soon at night'

Love is seen as a force for change.

Love can be physical and vulgar (rude).

Love

Love is seen as passionate and overwhelming.

Does love triumph over violence?

'O she doth teach the torches to burn bright!'

Yes: 'As rich shall Romeo's by his lady's lie/Poor sacrifices of our enmity'. The play concludes with Capulet's symbol of friendship and **resolution** of the conflict.

The beautiful **metaphor** captures Romeo's passion and his enthusiasm is illustrated in the **plosive** 'b' sounds.

No: At the end, Capulet seems to be still concerned about his status against the Montagues. The violence may well continue.

Sample GCSE Exam Question

Read the following extract from Act 2 Scene 2 of 'Romeo and Juliet'.

Answer both questions below the text.

At this point in the play, Romeo and Juliet are falling in love on the balcony after meeting at the Capulets' party.

ROMEO:
O, wilt thou leave me so unsatisfied?
JULIET:
What satisfaction canst thou have to-night?
ROMEO:
The exchange of thy love's faithful vow for mine.
JULIET:
I gave thee mine before thou didst request it:
And yet I would it were to give again.
ROMEO:
Wouldst thou withdraw it? for what purpose, love?
JULIET:
But to be frank, and give it thee again.
And yet I wish but for the thing I have:
My bounty is as boundless as the sea,
My love as deep; the more I give to thee,
The more I have, for both are infinite.

a) Discuss how love is presented in this extract.

b) Discuss how love is presented in the play as a whole.

 # Sample GCSE Answer

 Start with an overview

Love is at the centre of the play and drives much of the action as Shakespeare uses the characters to explore the many different aspects of love. In this extract, the audience watches in delight as the romantic love develops between the two protagonists yet other types of love are also presented in the play: filial love, carnal love and the platonic affection of friendship are all part of the complex emotion that is love.

☑ Make the point that love is presented as a powerful and positive emotion

In the extract, Juliet claims that **'my bounty is as boundless as the sea/My love as deep'**. This nature *simile* reveals the strength of love through comparing it to the incredibly powerful sea, without boundaries or limits. She extends the *simile* to present love as generous and selfless, as **'infinite'**. In a play where selfish actions based on family honour and revenge abound, Juliet's words illustrate the more noble side to human emotions. This famous balcony scene is set in the cool of night; Shakespeare deliberately uses *setting* to highlight the pure emotions of love, sharply *juxtaposing* this scene with the vengeful tempers in the **'hot'** days that lead to violence and tragedy.

The communication between the two lovers presents love as something which brings great joy. Romeo asks why she would **'withdraw it? for what purpose, love?'** and Juliet replies **'but to be frank, and give it thee again.'** Communication is easy and warm; the endearment **'love'** is tender and respectful. Juliet's answer is humorous yet also shows how she seeks to please Romeo and herself through the joy of commitment. This joy is shown when Romeo first sees Juliet and exclaims **'O she doth teach the torches to burn bright!'** Love is seen as an overwhelming and positive emotion. The *metaphor* is a spontaneous outburst of passion while the *plosive* **'b'** sounds capture Romeo's passion and enthusiasm. The *metaphor* also associates Juliet with light, a positive *image* showing her to be dazzling. Light is a *symbol* of hope which conveys to us that love is a force for good in the violence of Verona.

Juliet asks **'what satisfaction canst thou have to-night?'** She is referring to the physical satisfaction that she thinks Romeo has asked for- and denying it. Sex outside marriage would be outside the boundaries of acceptable behaviour in the Elizabethan era and Shakespeare again is showing their love to be true and pure. Romeo sees himself as profane (not religious) but improves himself and blesses himself when he touches Juliet's hand upon first meeting her. This reflects the conflict between the profane and the sacred in the play. Juliet is constantly seen as pure and sacred with religious *imagery* such as **'bright angel'** used to describe her. Romeo is seen as more down-to-earth. This is reflected in the *staging* of the balcony scene when Juliet is above Romeo. The conflict between the profane and the secular is reconciled when Romeo and Juliet are married and so have the blessing of the Church and so love is presented as a pure and elevating emotion which improves Romeo.

Later, safely married, Juliet is allowed to show her sexual side in her *soliloquy*: 'spread thy close curtain, **love-performing night'**, the *imperative verb* capturing her impatience to enjoy her wedding night. The Nurse is also used to show the more physical side to love with her bawdy language, for example, in the *pun* **'you shall bear the burden soon at night'**. Shakespeare's original audience would have enjoyed the play on words and the bawdy humour. In the theatre, the audience would have been fidgeting and chatting so humour would have been a device to hold their attention.

Love and violence are seen as two sides of the same coin. Even the lovers' wedding day is underscored with references to death as Friar Lawrence's words warn of the explosive nature of love, cautioning that **'these violent delights have violent ends'**. The *repetition* of the word **'violent'** issues a warning to the characters and to us. One of the themes of the play is that of conflict and clashes and the need to reconcile opposing forces; love and violence/hatred are in direct opposition throughout the play and are only reconciled at the end. Although the play ends with the tragic suicides, Romeo and Juliet's love has ensured peace and harmony in Verona. Capulet promises to pay for a statue of Romeo that will match Montague's statue of Juliet, saying **'as rich shall Romeo's by his lady's lie/Poor sacrifices of our enmity'**. *Structurally*, the Prologue's warning that the deaths will **'bury their parents' strife'** is now evident. Shakespeare uses the classic five act structure of a Greek tragedy to end with the *resolution*; with Capulet's symbol of friendship, the audience feels a sense of *catharsis* and closure, and this is emphasised with the use of *rhyming couplets* **'lie/enmity'**. Love has ensured that the violence in Verona is over. Yet an audience might question whether love has really triumphed. Capulet only mentions the statue of Romeo because Montague states how he intends to raise a statue of pure gold for Juliet first; this is a clear attempt to upstage his old foe. Even at the end, in the midst of the death and grief, Capulet seems to be concerned about his status against the Montagues and not his daughter. It makes the audience wonder whether the feud is really settled and buried or whether there will be future conflict; it seems that the love of Romeo and Juliet will be forgotten.

10 Tragedy
Exploration of a theme

'Romeo and Juliet' is one of the most famous stories of ill-fated love ever told. The ending is so tragic that it was re-written several times in the Victorian era so that it was not so painful to watch.

'pair of star-crossed lovers take their life'

- In the Prologue, the chorus clearly warns us that this is a tragedy.

- By telling us the ending of the play, the audience is aware from the very beginning that they will be watching a story of pain, conflict and death. It is a compelling and dramatic opening.

Context: The Elizabethan audience would have firmly believed in predetermination, that our lives are set out for us. They would have enjoyed watching the plot shape events towards the inevitable tragic ending.

'a plague a' both your houses'

- Mercutio curses both the Capulets and the Montagues after he is fatally stabbed by Tybalt. He places the blame for the violence which has resulted in his own death on both of the households.

- The negative **vocabulary** and the violence of this scene reflect the pain and conflict within Verona. The **pathetic fallacy** of this scene, with the **'hot'** day matching the hot tempers, creates a tense atmosphere which heightens the sense of tragedy.

- **Structurally**, Mercutio's curse is seen to be immediately effective in Act 3 as Romeo murders Tybalt and is banished, leading to the fatal end of the play.

'Susan is with God/She was too good for me'

- The Nurse speaks of her own baby's death with acceptance and grace.

- If tragedy means events that bring pain, then there are many examples in the play of the suffering of the minor characters. The Nurse has lost her baby and husband; the servant is powerless because he cannot read; the apothecary is so poor that he cannot afford a conscience. These low-born characters also suffer but their suffering is seen as a way of life. Perhaps Shakespeare was making a point that suffering is universal but the poor are far more stoic (strong).

'violently as hasty powder fired'

- When he hears of the 'death' of Juliet, Romeo seeks a swift death himself by drinking deadly poison.

- This impulsive behaviour, acting quickly without thinking things through, ensures that he plays a part in his own death.

- Shakespeare is drawing on conventions from Greek tragedy where the noble hero has a fatal flaw or **hamartia** that is his downfall. Romeo's fault or **hamartia** is his recklessness, the way he has of acting without thinking his actions through.

Context: Shakespeare explores in his plays the idea of self-determination; that our own decisions and choices cause us to follow the path fate has set for us. Romeo plays a part in his own tragic downfall.

'All are punished'

- At the end of the play, the Prince tells the assembled crowd and the audience that everyone has been hurt by the tragedy. Perhaps this is the definition of tragedy, that everyone has felt the pain and horror of the events.

- This short emphatic **statement** rings very true and **contrasts** to some of the Prince's more formal, elaborate speeches which give him a pompous air. This line is genuine and heart-felt, and he includes himself in the punishment as he, too, has lost family members. The tragedy affects all the characters.

Context: Shakespeare uses the classic five act **structure** and conventions of Greek tragedy to tell the story of 'Romeo and Juliet'. As the Prince acknowledges at the end that all are suffering, there is a sense of **catharsis** (cleansing) and **resolution**, that mistakes have been made and will be learnt from. The suffering will not have been in vain.

Grade 9 Exploration:
Look at the theme in a different way

Is the play a tragedy only after Act 3?

Yes: Up to Mercutio's death, Shakespeare provides us with a whole array of comic moments. From the very opening of Act 1, there is good-humoured banter amongst the men servants who make plenty of sexual jokes. Even the theme of love is mocked with Romeo moodily moping around after the untouchable Rosaline. The turning point of the play comes with the death of Mercutio and interestingly, humour is used here to accentuate the tragedy as Mercutio calls out **'ask for me tomorrow and you shall find me a grave man'**. This *pun* creates a sense of black humour here (**'grave**' means serious and also means being buried after dying), illustrating his bright intelligence and sense of wit; Mercutio's mind is able to use *wordplay* even as his body fails him. This is black comedy as the humour is heavily tainted with the pain of this scene and this highlights the tragedy of his death and that of Tybalt's. Mercutio's death marks an end to the comic elements to the play; pain, suffering and death dominate the rest of the play.

No: From the opening, the Prologue works like a Greek chorus did in warning us that we are about to watch a tragedy in which **'star-cross'd lovers take their life'**, and this sense of fate cuts through all the comic moments. Even the early comedy of the men servants quickly evaporates into the brawl that has Tybalt announce **'peace? I hate the word, as I hate hell, all Montagues and thee'**, revealing his dark corrosive hatred that weaves itself through the play. The violence and menace prepare us right from the beginning of Act 1 that we are watching a tragedy.

Much of the drama of the Elizabethan period mixed elements of classical comedy with the conventions of Greek tragedy; Shakespeare was following this literary convention by weaving the comedy into the tragedy.

Essential Exam Tips

☑ Try watching different versions of the play to see how different directors present themes and characters.

☑ To write about Greek tragedy, with its conventions of *hamartia*, *catharsis* and *resolution*, is a good way to reach higher marks; try to use these points in your answer.

By having this foreknowledge that the lovers will die, we are constantly aware of the relentless presence of fate throughout the play.

'Pair of star-crossed lovers take their life'

In the Prologue, the chorus clearly warns us that this is a tragedy.

Romeo's impetuous nature is his *hamartia*; his impulsive behaviour ensures that he plays a part in the tragedy.

'violently as hasty powder fired'

The characters' actions contribute to the tragic ending.

Tragedy

The Prince acknowledges that everyone is suffering the pain of the tragedy.

'All are punished'

At the end, there is a sense of *catharsis* and of *resolution* in that mistakes have been made and will be learnt from.

Is the tragedy of the play weakened by the comedy?

Yes: Even the very opening of Act 1 is full of sexual jokes amongst the men servants and the theme of love is mocked with Romeo's moody moping.

No: There is real hate from the start. Tybalt's words **'peace? I hate the word, as I hate hell, all Montagues and thee'** reveals the dark hatred that causes the tragedy.

Read the following extract from Act 5 Scene 3 of 'Romeo and Juliet'.

Answer both questions below the text.

At this point in the play, the dead bodies of the lovers have been found and the Prince is concluding the play.

PRINCE:
See, what a scourge is laid upon your hate,
That heaven finds means to kill your joys with love.
And I for winking at your discords too
Have lost a brace of kinsmen: all are punish'd.

CAPULET:
O brother Montague, give me thy hand:
This is my daughter's jointure, for no more
Can I demand.

MONTAGUE:
But I can give thee more:
For I will raise her statue in pure gold;
That while Verona by that name is known,
There shall no figure at such rate be set
As that of true and faithful Juliet.

CAPULET:
As rich shall Romeo's by his lady's lie;
Poor sacrifices of our enmity!

PRINCE:
A glooming peace this morning with it brings;
The sun, for sorrow, will not show his head:
Go hence, to have more talk of these sad things;
Some shall be pardon'd, and some punished:
For never was a story of more woe
Than this of Juliet and her Romeo.

a) Discuss how the idea of tragedy is presented in this extract.

b) Discuss how the idea of tragedy is presented in the play as a whole.

Sample GCSE Answer

☑ Start with an overview

'Romeo and Juliet' is one of the most famous stories of ill-fated love ever told and in the extract the audience watches the painful last scene as the full horror of the double suicides unfolds. This ending is so tragic that it was re-written several times in the Victorian era so that it was not so agonising to watch; certainly the play is skilfully crafted by Shakespeare to reveal the devastating pain that conflict brings.

☑ Make the point that the suffering at the end is universal

At the end of the play, the Prince tells the assembled crowd and the audience that everyone has been hurt by the tragedy as **'all are punished'**. The word **'all'** encompasses every character and reminds the Montagues and the Capulets that their feud has damaged everyone, reinforcing the message that violent hatred leads to tragedy. Perhaps this is the definition of tragedy, that everyone has felt the pain and horror of the events. This short emphatic **statement** rings very true and **contrasts** with some of his more formal, elaborate speeches which give him a pompous air. This line is genuine and heart-felt, and he includes himself in the punishment as he has, too, lost family members. Shakespeare uses Greek tragedy and its conventions to **structure** his tragedy and, as the Prince acknowledges that all are suffering, there is a sense of **catharsis** (cleansing) and a **resolution** for the audience in that mistakes have been made and will be learnt from.

✓ Make the point that the language creates a sense of genuine tragedy

The **personification** of the sun mourning the dead lovers in the line **'the sun for sorrow will not show its head'** highlights the scale of this tragedy. Even the cosmos (universe) is affected by the deaths of such young lovers, and with the sun in mourning there is a sense of deep mourning and darkness, both metaphorical and literal. **Rhyming couplets** in this final speech help give the play a sense of **resolution** and conclusion. The Prince's words conclude the play; this fitted in with the literary convention of the time. It is significant that the final words are given to the most senior figure, acknowledging his authority and emphasising that his judgement, that this story is one of tragic woe, is correct. The prince uses the language of **contrast** 'love/hate' in the lines **'what a scourge is laid upon your hate/That heaven finds means to kill your joys with love.'** This language reflects the cause of the tragedy, that of conflict and clashes and the need to reconcile opposing forces. It is the lack of harmony that creates the tension and leads to the tragic ending; only with the death of the true lovers can peace and balance come to Verona.

✓ Explore who is to blame for the tragedy

When he hears of the 'death' of Juliet, Romeo seeks a swift death himself by drinking deadly poison. This impulsive behaviour, acting quickly without thinking things through, ensures that he plays a part in his own death. Shakespeare is drawing on conventions from Greek tragedy when the noble hero has a fatal flaw or **hamartia** that is his downfall. Romeo's fault or **hamartia** is his recklessness, the way he has of acting quickly without thinking his actions through. Shakespeare explores in his plays the idea of self-determination; that our own decisions and choices cause us to create our own destiny. Yet this view differs to the typical Elizabethan view of predetermination, that our lives are set out for us by fate and we cannot avoid tragedy. This sense of fate being to blame for the tragedy is shown with Mercutio **repetitively** shouting **'a plague o' both your houses'**; immediately, this curse is seen working as Tybalt is killed and Romeo banished.

✓ Explore how tragedy is presented alongside comedy

Much of the drama of the Elizabethan period mixed elements of classical comedy with the conventions of Greek tragedy; Shakespeare was following this literary convention by weaving humour into the story. An example of this is in Act 3 when the use of **puns** showcase Mercutio's wit. The black humour of **'ask for me tomorrow and you shall find me a grave man'** ('**grave**' means serious and also means being buried as he will be dead) illustrates his bright intelligence and sense of wit; his mind is able to use **wordplay** even as his body fails him. This is black comedy; the comedy is heavily tainted with the pain of this scene and Shakespeare uses this black comedy to highlight the tragedy of his death and that of Tybalt's. Some critics argue that the sense of tragedy in 'Romeo and Juliet' is weakened by an excess of humour. In the first two acts, up until Mercutio's death, Shakespeare provides us with a whole array of comic moments; right from the beginning of the play, there are lots of sexual jokes amongst the men servants. Even the theme of love is mocked with Romeo moodily moping around after the untouchable Rosaline. However, the Prologue works like a Greek chorus in warning us that we are to watch a tragedy in which **'star-cross'd lovers take their life'**, and this sense of Fate cuts through all the comic moments. Even the early comedy of the men servants quickly evaporates into the brawl that has Tybalt announce **'peace? I hate the word, as I hate hell, all Montagues and thee'**, revealing his dark corrosive hatred that weaves itself through the play. The violence and menace prepare us right from Act 1 that we are watching a tragedy and it would be hard to argue with the play's final words, that **'never was there a story of more woe than that of Juliet and her Romeo'**.

Comedy

Exploration of the text

'Romeo and Juliet' is regarded as one of the most famous tragedies ever written. However, Shakespeare also weaves comedy through the story in a number of ways.

'A crutch! A crutch! Why call you for a sword?'

- There is comedy right at the start as Lady Capulet taunts her ageing husband who is desperate to fight.
- This is a humorous moment which serves to highlight the very real, serious violence of the opening fight.
- Shakespeare uses humour here to raise one of the themes of the play: youth versus age. Lady Capulet is much younger than her husband and the difference in ages could be the cause of the lack of warmth between them.

'She'll not be hit/ With Cupid's arrow, she hath Diana's wit'

- The audience sees Romeo's immaturity as he sighs over Rosaline, his love based on a passion for a woman he barely knows.
- Shakepeare is inviting us to laugh at human folly (foolishness) by presenting us with the self-indulgent Romeo whose **hyperbolic** praising of Rosaline is every cliche of a love-struck young man.

Context: He relies heavily on the **Petrarchan language** of courtly love when a man worships a lady from afar, writing love poems to a woman he cannot get close to. The audience would have recognised the style and have been entertained by it.

'I am sent to find those persons whose names here are writ'

- The servant provides humour as he is given the job of handing out party invitations but cannot read. This is an example of **situational irony** and ends with completely the wrong people being invited; the Montagues are coming to the Capulets' feast.
- The servant uses **prose** which fits with the literary tradition of the time; **prose** was used by comic characters and those of low birth.

Context: Shakespeare uses the humour to make a serious point: that illiteracy strips people of power and makes them objects of fun. Illiteracy was common amongst the poor in Elizabethan society. Humour is perhaps used to comment on society's problems.

| **'You shall bear the burden soon at night'** | • Nurse uses **puns**, making crude sexual reference to Juliet's wedding night.

• Shakespeare uses the Nurse as a **contrast** to the purity of the young lovers' feelings for each other, showing the physical side to love. | **Context:** Shakespeare's original audience would have enjoyed the play on words and the bawdy humour. In the theatre, the audience would have been standing in front of the stage, fidgeting and chatting, so humour would have been a device to hold their attention. |

| **'that she were an open-arse, thou a pop'rin pear'** | • Mercutio uses sexual innuendo to tease Romeo, choosing vulgar (rude) **vocabulary** and reference to a fruit that looks like genitalia. The actor playing Mercutio would also certainly be using his body and facial expressions to make the most of the comic lines. Similarly, the long **vowel** sounds of **'open arse'** and the short, jaunty (cheerful) **alliteration** of the **'p'** in **'pop'rin pear'** lend themselves to comic acting and the amusement of the audience. |

• This scene is especially amusing because of the **dramatic irony**; the audience knows that Romeo has headed off to find Juliet so cannot hear the sexual innuendos made at his expense.

• **Structurally**, there is a **contrast** here between the coarse, sexual love that Mercutio is describing with the true, devoted love of Romeo in the next balcony scene. This **contrast** highlights both the humour and the romance.

| **'Ask for me tomorrow and you shall find me a grave man'** | • The use of a **pun** reflects Mercutio's wit, even as he dies.

• The black humour here (**'grave'** means serious and also means being buried after dying) illustrates his bright intelligence and sense of wit; his mind is able to use **wordplay** even as his body fails him. This is black comedy as the humour is heavily tainted with the pain of this scene. |

• Shakespeare uses this black comedy to highlight the tragedy of his death and that of Tybalt's.

• Mercutio's death marks an end to the comic elements to the play. Pain, suffering and death dominate the rest of the play.

Grade 9 Exploration:
Look at the theme in a different way

Is the play up to Act 3 more of a comedy than a tragedy?

Yes: Up to Mercutio's death, Shakespeare provides us with a whole array of comic moments; from the the very opening of Act 1, there are sexual jokes amongst the men servants. Shakespeare even mocks the theme of love with Romeo moodily moping around after the untouchable Rosaline.

No: The Prologue works as a Greek chorus in warning us that we are to watch a tragedy in which **'star-cross'd lovers take their life'**, and this sense of fate cuts through all the comic moments. Even the early comedy of the men servants quickly evaporates into the brawl that ends with Tybalt announcing **'peace? I hate the word, as I hate hell, all Montagues and thee'**, revealing his dark corrosive hatred that weaves itself through the play.

Much of the drama of the Elizabethan period mixed elements of classical comedy with the conventions of Greek tragedy; Shakespeare was following this literary convention by weaving the comedy into the tragedy.

Essential Exam Tips

- ☑ The context box above is the same as the previous chapter. When you are revising the comedy and tragedy, some of the points can be 'recycled'. This makes revision very focused.

- ☑ When you read the extract, try to visualise the scene as you've seen it acted on stage or in a film. This will help you analyse ideas and characters.

- ☑ Don't try to write something about every single line in the extract; you don't have time! Focus on 4-5 different words/phrases only.

Shakespeare uses the humour to illustrate how literacy strips people of power and makes them objects of fun.

This bawdy (rude) joke about sex on Juliet's wedding night serves two purposes: 1) entertainment 2) It *contrasts* with the pure romantic love of Romeo and Juliet.

'I am sent to find those persons whose names here are writ'

'You shall bear the burden soon at night'

There is *situational irony* with the servant who hands out invitations and ends up inviting the hated Montagues to the Capulets' feast.

Shakespeare uses the Nurse as a comic character to amuse the audience.

Comedy

The use of a *pun* shows Mercutio's wit even as he dies.

Is the play up to Act 3 more of a comedy than a tragedy?

'Ask for me tomorrow and you shall find me a grave man'

Yes: The very opening of Act 1 is full of sexual jokes amongst the men servants. Even the theme of love is mocked with Romeo moodily moping around after the untouchable Rosaline.

Shakespeare uses this black comedy to highlight the tragedy of the deaths of Mercutio and Tybalt.

No: The Prologue works as a Greek chorus to tell us very clearly that we are watching a tragedy. Even the early comedy of the men servants quickly evaporates into a violent brawl.

Read the following extract from Act 2 Scene 4 of 'Romeo and Juliet'.

Answer both questions below the text.

At this point in the play, the Nurse is looking for Romeo to arrange his marriage to Juliet.

Enter NURSE and PETER

MERCUTIO:
A sail, a sail!

BENVOLIO:
Two, two; a shirt and a smock.

NURSE:
Peter!

PETER:
Anon!

NURSE:
My fan, Peter.

MERCUTIO:
Good Peter, to hide her face; for her fan's the fairer face.

NURSE:
God ye good morrow, gentlemen.

MERCUTIO:
God ye good den, fair gentlewoman.

NURSE:
Is it good den?

MERCUTIO:
'Tis no less, I tell you, for the bawdy hand of the dial is now upon the prick of noon.

NURSE
Out upon you! what a man are you!

a) Write about how comedy is used in this extract.

b) Write about how comedy is used in the play as a whole.

 # Sample GCSE Answer

☑ Start with an overview

'Romeo and Juliet' is regarded as one of the most famous tragedies ever written. However, Shakespeare also weaves comedy through the story in a number of ways and this humour is evident here as the Nurse sweeps self-importantly into the male gathering and becomes the target of Mercutio's witty banter.

☑ Make the point that the Nurse and Mercutio are in part comic characters

In the extract, Shakespeare is using both Mercutio and the Nurse as comic devices to add humour to the play. There is visual comedy in the representation of the Nurse who obviously looks ridiculous; Mercutio's melodramatic nautical **vocabulary 'a sail! a sail!'** to describe the Nurse as an approaching ship implies that her clothes are billowing around her and this melodramatic language is then humorously undercut by Benvolio's pragmatic (everyday) detail of what she is actually wearing which is **'a shirt and a smock'**. The use of this contrasting **vocabulary** and the visual comedy create an entertaining entrance for the Nurse.

✓ Develop this point that the Nurse continues to entertain

More visual comedy is created with the Nurse calling to her servant for her **'fan'**. In Elizabethan times, fans were often so large as to need someone to carry them; a good comic actor could do much with this oversized fan. There is humour too in the Nurse putting on airs and graces by carrying a fan and having a servant. She is just a servant herself yet is full of her own importance. The humour continues as Mercutio flirts with her and flusters her. The whole exchange is in **prose** which follows the literary convention of the time as **prose** was used for comic moments. The quick interchange of banter helps both create humour and increase the pace of the scene so that it's lively and entertaining. This was a device used by Shakespeare to keep his audience engaged; this quick-fire comic scene is **juxtaposed** with the previous slower scene of Friar Lawrence and Romeo planning the wedding.

✓ Make the point that Mercutio often uses sexual humour

Mercutio immediately cracks a vulgar (dirty) joke, saying **'tis no less, I tell you, for the bawdy hand of the dial is now upon the prick of noon'**, crudely and graphically using a **metaphor** that links time with masturbation. Shakespeare's original audience would have enjoyed the play on words and the bawdy (sexual) humour. In the theatre, the audience would have been standing in front of the stage, fidgeting and chatting, so humour would have been a device to hold their attention. Mercutio's coarse view of love also serves to **contrast** with Romeo's pure love. Mercutio's sexual innuendos in Act 2 are very entertaining with the long **vowel sound** of '**open arse**' and the short, jaunty **alliteration** of **'pop'rin pear'** lending themselves to comic acting. This comic banter highlights the purity of the lovers in the balcony scene which follows.

✓ Move to a different part in the play where Shakespeare uses literary conventions to invite us to laugh at human nature

In Act 1, Romeo is moping over the unattainable (unreachable) Rosaline **'she'll not be hit/With Cupid's arrow, she hath Diana's wit.'** The audience sees Romeo's immaturity here, his love based on a passion for a woman he barely knows, and would enjoy this melodramatic languishing on Romeo's part. The **rhyming couplets** 'hit/wit' strike an artificial note which also amuses us. Shakepeare is inviting us to laugh at human folly (foolishness) by showing us the self-indulgent Romeo whose **hyperbolic** praising of Rosaline is every cliche of a love-struck young man. He relies heavily on the **Petrarchan language** of courtly love when a man worships a lady from afar, writing love poems to a woman he cannot get close to. The audience would have recognised the style and have been entertained by it.

✓ Explore how far comedy can be seen as a defining feature of 'Romeo and Juliet'

It is interesting to consider whether the play up to Act 3 is more of a comedy than a tragedy. It would seem so as, up to Mercutio's death, Shakespeare provides us with a whole array of comic moments with the very opening of Act 1 full of sexual jokes amongst the men servants. Even the theme of love is mocked with Romeo moodily moping around after the untouchable Rosaline. Yet the comedy is constantly tainted with a darker edge. The Prologue works as a Greek chorus in warning us from the opening that we are to watch a tragedy in which **'star-cross'd lovers take their life'** and this sense of fate cuts through all the comic moments. Even the early comedy of the men servants quickly evaporates into the brawl that has Tybalt announce '**Peace? I hate the word, as I hate hell, all Montagues and thee'**, revealing his dark corrosive hatred that weaves itself through the play. And from Act 3 onwards, there is no comedy; just a sense of unfolding tragedy that the characters and the audience are powerless to prevent.

'Romeo and Juliet' is a play that is full of tension, with Shakespeare using many dramatic devices (techniques) to ensure that the audience is fully engaged.

'pair of star-crossed lovers take their life'

- In the Prologue, the chorus clearly warns us that this play is a tragedy.

- By telling us the ending of the play, the audience is aware from the very beginning that they will be watching a story of pain, conflict and death. It is a compelling and dramatic opening.

Context: The chorus is a literary device used by ancient Greek playwrights and by Shakespeare to guide the audience response. By having this foreknowledge that the lovers will die, we are constantly aware of the relentless presence of fate throughout the play and are implicitly (completely) involved in the couple's doomed relationship, which creates unease and tension for the audience.

'The day is hot, the Capulets are abroad/If we meet we shall not scape a brawl'

- Benvolio, the peacemaker, gives us clear warning that trouble is coming.

- Shakespeare uses **contrast** to sharply escalate the tension. The previous scene is that of Romeo and Juliet's wedding with its gentle harmonious atmosphere. The marriage represents the ultimate in harmony. There is immediate **juxtaposition** with the busy city centre here and Benvolio's anxiety clearly evident.

- The **pathetic fallacy** of the **'hot'** weather reflects the high tempers of the men and the atmosphere is charged with fractious violence, **foreshadowing** the fight scene that soon follows.

'O calm dishonourable vile submission'

- Mercutio cannot understand Romeo's refusal to fight with Tybalt. His language reflects his disgust at Romeo's peace-keeping and the **triplet** of **adjectives** shows his growing anger which soon explodes, adding to the tension.

- There is **dramatic irony** here as the audience has knowledge that Mercutio does not; Romeo is not fighting because he has just married Juliet, Tybalt's cousin. Shakespeare uses **dramatic irony** to create tension; we understand the character's emotions and actions but they react to each other without the knowledge that the audience has. It makes the unnecessary deaths of Mercutio and Tybalt more dramatic and more painful because we fully understand how needless they are.

Context: The notion of masculine honour was very important in Elizabethan society; the audience would understand Mercutio's outrage at allowing an insult to go undefended.

'as one dead in the bottom of a tomb'

- Juliet looks down at Romeo as he leaves their wedding bed for Mantua and has a frightening vision of seeing him dead. This is **foreshadowing**; the next time she sees Romeo he is indeed dead in the Capulet's vault. The **foreshadowing** works to build tension; the audience is reminded that death and violence stalk this couple and the constant references to graves and death reinforce this. The audience is never allowed to relax and enjoy the passionate love affair as we are always tensely waiting for things to go wrong.

- There is sharp **juxtaposition** here between the passion of their wedding night and the joy it has brought them and this grim, unsettling vision, making the audience keenly feel the **pathos** of their doomed love.

Context: The Elizabethan audience would have firmly believed in predetermination, that our lives are set out for us, and that Juliet cannot escape the sad fate that is planned for herself and her Romeo.

> 'Out you baggage! You tallow-face!'

- Tension is created here through the violence of Capulet's language and the conflict erupting within the family unit.

- Capulet's hasty temper explodes here as he attacks Juliet for refusing to marry Paris. His fury is seen in the short, emphatic sentences. The range of insults used in this scene shows an unbalanced reaction to his daughter.

- The language is vicious. **'Baggage'** implies a woman of loose morals, **'tallow'** relates to the animal fat in candle wax; he is definitely hurling deliberate insults at her and the ***imperative verb*** **'out'** shows the sense of commanding entitlement he has.

- The tension created here is obvious through the violent conflict, but also through the ***dramatic irony***. The audience is fully aware why it is impossible for Juliet to marry Paris (she is already married to Romeo) yet the other characters act without this knowledge, which creates a tense scene.

Grade 9 Exploration:
Look at the theme in a different way

Does the ending bring resolution to the dramatic conflict?

Yes: The Prince concludes the play with the lines **'for never was a story of more woe/Than this of Juliet and her Romeo'**; the ***rhyming couplets*** **'woe/Romeo'** in this final speech help give the play a sense of ***resolution*** and conclusion. The tension dissipates (disappears) and a sense of peace and calm is established in Verona.

No: Capulet promises to raise a statue for Romeo, declaring **'as rich shall Romeo's by his lady's lie/Poor sacrifices of our enmity'**. However, he only mentions this because Montague states how he intends to raise a statue of pure gold for Juliet first; this is a clear attempt to maintain status against his old foe. Even at the end, in the midst of the death and grief, Capulet seems to be concerned about his status against the Montagues and not his daughter. It makes the audience wonder whether the feud is really settled and buried or whether there will be future conflict- the tension is held right until the end.

Shakespeare uses the classic five act ***structure*** of Greek tragedy to control the tension. This means that in the final act, the characters reach a point of ***resolution*** and the audience feels a sense of ***catharsis*** (cleansing) in that lessons have been learnt from the tragedy.

Essential Exam Tip

☑ Shakespeare does not use many stage directions; if they are used, do see if you can comment on them. Stage directions form part of Shakespeare's dramatic techniques so do analyse them if you can.

By having this foreknowledge that the lovers will die, we are always aware of the relentless presence of fate throughout the play which builds tension.

Benvolio's anxiety infects the audience; the **'hot'** days reflect the hot tempers, reminding us of the violence that always threatens to erupt in Verona's streets.

'pair of star-crossed lovers take their life'

'The day is hot, the Capulets are abroad/ And if we meet we shall not scape a brawl'

In the Prologue, the chorus clearly warns us that this play is a tragedy.

Shakespeare uses *pathetic fallacy* to create tension.

Drama & Tension

Juliet's vision of the dead Romeo uses foreshadowing to create tension.

Is the tension resolved at the end of the play?

'as one dead in the bottom of a tomb'

Yes: 'As rich shall Romeo's by his lady's lie/Poor sacrifices of our enmity'. The play concludes with Capulet's *symbol* of friendship; a sense of peace and calm is created.

The audience is reminded that death and violence stalk this couple and the constant references to graves and death reinforce this.

No: At the end, Capulet seems to be still concerned about his status against the Montagues and not his daughter. Tensions between the families continue.

Read the following extract from Act 3 Scene 1 of 'Romeo and Juliet'.

Answer both questions below the text.

At this point in the play, Mercutio is challenging Tybalt to a fight.

MERCUTIO:
Good king of cats, nothing but one of your nine
lives; that I mean to make bold withal, and as you
shall use me hereafter, drybeat the rest of the
eight. Will you pluck your sword out of his pitcher
by the ears? make haste, lest mine be about your
ears ere it be out.

TYBALT:
I am for you. (Drawing)

ROMEO:
Gentle Mercutio, put thy rapier up.

MERCUTIO:
Come, sir, your passado.
They fight

ROMEO:
Draw, Benvolio; beat down their weapons.
Gentlemen, for shame, forbear this outrage!
Tybalt, Mercutio, the prince expressly hath
Forbidden bandying in Verona streets:
Hold, Tybalt! good Mercutio!
TYBALT under ROMEO's arm stabs MERCUTIO, and flies with his followers

a) How are drama and tension created in this extract?

b) How are drama and tension created in the play as a whole?

 # Sample GCSE Answer

☑ Start with an overview

'Romeo and Juliet' is a play that is full of tension, with Shakespeare using many dramatic devices (techniques) to ensure that the audience is fully engaged. This extract is a pivotal scene as the fight sets in motion the fatal chain of events that leads to the double suicide, and the dramatic tension of Mercutio and Tybalt's fight is created and maintained so that the audience watches in constant suspense.

☑ Make the point that drama and tension are created through the visual conflict

The **stage directions** 'stab', 'drawing', **'flies'** create a sense of high drama with the dynamic **verbs** clearly being used to maximise the tension; the violence of the scene is clearly visible here to the audience. Shakespeare also uses **contrast** to sharply escalate the tension. The previous scene is that of Romeo and Juliet's wedding with its gentle, harmonious atmosphere. The marriage represents the ultimate in harmony and there is immediate **juxtaposition** with this busy city centre in the hot day, as the hot tempers now spill over into aggressive physical violence.

Make the point that the language creates a sense of drama and tension

Mercutio deliberately goads Tybalt, calling him **'king of cats'**. Referring to him in this way reminds us that Tybalt has a reputation for excellent swordsmanship and this increases the tension as we know the scene could turn deadly. Yet there is humour in the teasing as Mercutio taunts Tybalt to pull out his sword, saying **'will you pluck your sword out of his pitcher by the ears? make haste, lest mine be about your ears ere it be out.'** He is speaking in **prose**, which literary convention dictated was used for comedy, and his sharp wit is shown in the **wordplay** on **'ears'**. Elizabethan audiences were fascinated by **wordplay** and would have enjoyed the punning here. Again, Shakespeare uses contrast to ramp up the tension; this time there is a shift from Mercutio's comic speech to Romeo's use of **iambic pentameter** and **blank verse** as he tries to halt the violence. Romeo's language is clearly frantic; the short, **exclamatory sentences** such as **'hold, Tybalt!'** capture his sense of urgency, as do the many **imperative verbs** used **'draw' 'beat' 'hold'** as Romeo desperately seeks to stop the fight.

 Make the point that the tension is created through suspense

Romeo gives a good reason to stop the fighting, that **'the prince expressly hath/ Forbidden bandying in Verona streets'**. He reminds the audience that the Prince has pronounced a death sentence on anyone caught fighting and so reminds us that this fight is deadly serious, no matter who wins. By referring to the Prince, the absolute authority in Verona, Shakespeare explores the theme of opposites, that of the individual versus society, showing us how conflict is created when individual needs do not coincide with society's needs and how this causes tension that needs to be resolved. **Dramatic irony** is also used as the audience knows about the recent wedding and understand Romeo's motivations in trying to stop the fight but the others react to each other without this knowledge. It makes the deaths of the men more dramatic and more painful because we understand how needless they are.

Explore how constant **foreshadowing** creates tension

In the Prologue, the chorus clearly warns us that this is a tragedy: **'a pair of star-cross'd lovers take their life'**. By telling us the end of the play, the audience is aware from the very beginning that they will be watching a story of pain, conflict and death. It is a compelling and dramatic opening. The chorus is a literary device used by ancient Greek playwrights and by Shakespeare to guide the audience response. By having this foreknowledge that the lovers will die, we are constantly aware of the relentless presence of fate throughout the play and are implicitly involved in the couple's doomed relationship, which creates an ongoing sense of drama. Shakespeare constantly reminds us of the fact that the lovers will die. Even on the morning after her wedding night, Juliet has a vision of Romeo **'as one dead in the bottom of a tomb'**. There is sharp **juxtaposition** here between the passion and vibrancy of their wedding night and the joy it has brought them and this grim, unsettling vision, making the audience feel the pathos (sadness) of their doomed love. This is **foreshadowing**; the next time she sees Romeo he is indeed dead in the Capulet's vault. The **foreshadowing** works to build tension; the audience is reminded that death and violence stalk this couple and the constant references to graves and death reinforce this. The Elizabethan audience would have firmly believed in predetermination, that our lives are set out for us and that Juliet cannot escape her sad fate. The tragic ending is inevitable and this adds to the tension.

Move to the ending of the play to examine whether the tension is resolved

The ending seems to bring **resolution** to the conflict as the Prince concludes the play with the lines **'for never was a story of more woe/Than this of Juliet and her Romeo'**; the **rhyming couplets** in this final speech help give the play a sense of **resolution** and conclusion. The tension dissipates and a sense of peace and calm is established in Verona. Yet, although Capulet promises to raise a statue for Romeo, declaring **'as rich shall Romeo's by his lady's lie/Poor sacrifices of our enmity'**, he only mentions this because Montague states how he intends to raise a statue of pure gold for Juliet first. This is a clear attempt at one-upmanship. Even at the end, in the midst of the death and grief, Capulet seems to be concerned about his status against the Montagues and not his daughter. It makes the audience wonder whether the feud is really settled and buried or whether there will be future conflict; the tension is held right until the end.

'Romeo and Juliet' raises questions of how much free will we have over our actions. Do we have any choice at all? Or does fate determine how we live and when we die?

'pair of star-crossed lovers take their life'

- In the Prologue, the chorus warns us that Romeo and Juliet are **'star-cross'd'** and that there is nothing they can do to escape their fate of death.

- The chorus is a device used by ancient Greek playwrights and by Shakespeare to guide the audience's response. By having this foreknowledge that the lovers will die, we are constantly aware of the relentless presence of fate throughout the play and are implicitly (completely) involved in the couple's doomed relationship.

- Also, by telling us the end of the play, the audience is aware from the very beginning that they will be watching a story of pain, conflict and death. It is a compelling and dramatic opening.

- *Images* associating Juliet with **'light'** weave through the play: **'bright angel'**, **'she doth teach the torches to burn bright'**. These *images* constantly remind the audience that she is **'star-cross'd'**, creating a sense of unease and tension.

Context: Astrology, consulting the stars to see what the future would hold, was very popular in the Elizabethan era. The audience would have believed that the alignment (positioning) of the stars meant that the lovers were doomed.

'if he be married/ My grave is like to be my wedding bed'	• Juliet's words when she first meets Romeo are extreme; she will die if she cannot marry him. She, like Romeo, has been swept up in a storm of strong emotion, showing the intensity of true love, love that is doomed. • Shakespeare uses **foreshadowing**: the association here of love with death reminds us of the Prologue's warning that these lovers are doomed as **'star-cross'd'**. This **foreshadowing** works to remind us that death and violence stalk this couple and these constant references to graves and death reinforce this. The audience is never allowed to relax and enjoy the passionate love affair; we are always tensely waiting for fate to step in.

'I am sent to find those persons whose names here are writ'	• Fate is seen at work as the servant who cannot read approaches Romeo with the party invitations, leading to Romeo attending the Capulets' feast and meeting Juliet.	**Context:** The Elizabethan audience would have firmly believed in predetermination, that our lives are set out for us. They would have enjoyed watching the plot shape events towards the inevitable meeting of Romeo and Juliet.

'a plague a' both your houses'	• Mercutio's final words curse both the Montagues and Capulets. • **Structurally**, the curse is shown to be immediately effective as Romeo murders Tybalt and is banished, leading to the fateful end of the play. • Shakespeare does this to remind us of the relentless power of fate and how its path is consistently followed by all the characters.

'O fortune! all men call thee fickle'	• As Romeo leaves for Mantua, Juliet sees fate as having control over Romeo, being able to send him to places on a whim (fancy). • Juliet is refering here to Fortuna, the goddess of luck, who kept a wheel that determined one's happiness. A person could be at the top of the wheel, enjoying health and prosperity, but if Fortuna chose to spin her wheel, then life could change dramatically.

• When he hears of the 'death' of Juliet, Romeo seeks a swift death himself by drinking deadly poison.

• This impulsive behaviour, acting quickly without thinking things through, ensures that he plays a part in his own death.

• *Structurally*, we are reminded of Friar Lawrence's earlier warning about violent loves culminating (finishing) in violent ends; that prediction is now clearly played out in the apothecary's shop.

Context: In his plays, Shakespeare explored the idea of self-determination, that our own decisions and choices cause us to follow the path fate has set for us.

Grade 9 Exploration:
Look at the theme in a different way

Is fate entirely to blame for the tragedy?

Yes: From the beginning, the Prologue warns us that the lovers are **'star-cross'd'** and therefore doomed to die. There is nothing Romeo could do to avert his fate; by choosing suicide as his course of action, he merely plays into the hands of fate, becoming the first of the **'star-cross'd lovers'** to die.

No: Romeo hears about Juliet's death and shouts **'then I defy you, stars!'** He addresses the cold, unfeeling powers that govern his life and cause such grief; he recognises that fate has played its part in Juliet's death but decides to show his own power. By killing himself, he is taking back the last vestige of control, choosing his own place and time of death. Yet if Romeo had not been so hasty, if he had waited a few moments, then tragedy could have been averted. Shakespeare uses the Greek conventions of tragedy which means that the tragic hero (Romeo) has a *hamartia* (fatal flaw) which leads to his downfall; it is his fatal flaw of impetuousness that results in the lovers' deaths.

Essential Exam Tips

☑ Use formal language throughout your response.

☑ Some of the exam boards will assess your spelling, punctuation and grammar on this question. Even if these skills are not assessed, you do need to write as well as you can; check your work for errors.

Astrology - consulting the stars to see what the future would hold - was very popular in the Elizabethan era.

Frequent references to death and graves in the play constantly remind the audience that fate has grim plans for the couple.

'a pair of star-cross'd lover take their life'

'If he be married/My grave is like to be my wedding bed'

In the Prologue, the chorus warns us that Romeo and Juliet are doomed to die.

Foreshadowing is used to remind us that the characters will follow fate's path.

Fate & Fortune

Mercutio's words curse both families.

Is fate entirely to blame for the tragedy?

'a plague a' both your houses'

No: Romeo plays his own part, saying **'I defy you, stars!'** and choosing to kill himself.

Structurally, the curse is shown to be immediately effective as Romeo murders Tybalt and is banished, leading to the fatal end of the play.

Yes: Romeo thinks he is defying fate but by swallowing poison, he only follows the path of death that fate has set out for him.

Sample GCSE Exam Question

Read the following extract from Act 3 Scene 5 of 'Romeo and Juliet'.

Answer both questions below the text.

At this point in the play, Juliet is saying farewell to Romeo after their wedding night.

JULIET:
O God, I have an ill-divining soul!
Methinks I see thee, now thou art below,
As one dead in the bottom of a tomb:
Either my eyesight fails, or thou look'st pale.

ROMEO:
And trust me, love, in my eye so do you:
Dry sorrow drinks our blood. Adieu, adieu!
Exit

JULIET:
O fortune, fortune! all men call thee fickle:
If thou art fickle, what dost thou with him
That is renown'd for faith? Be fickle, fortune;
For then, I hope, thou wilt not keep him long,
But send him back.

a) Discuss how the idea of fate is presented in this extract.

b) Discuss how the idea of fate is presented in the play as a whole.

Sample GCSE Answer

☑ Start with an overview

'Romeo and Juliet' raises questions of how much free will we have over our actions. Do we have any choice at all? Or does fate determine how we live and when we die? In this extract, Juliet fears the powers of fate and desperately seeks to avert the vision of the future that she sees.

☑ Make the point that Juliet has a vision which warns her of Romeo's death

Juliet looks down at Romeo and has a frightening vision, seeing Romeo **'as one dead in the bottom of a tomb'**. This is **foreshadowing**; the next time she sees Romeo he is indeed dead in the Capulets' vault. There is sharp **juxtaposition** here between the passion and vibrancy of their wedding night and the joy it has brought them and this grim, unsettling vision, making the audience feel the **pathos** (sadness) of their doomed love. The audience is reminded that death and violence stalk this couple and the constant references to graves and death reinforce this.

☑ Develop this point that fate is a significant force in people's lives

Juliet's **exclamatory minor sentence**, **repeating** the words **'O fortune, fortune!'** shows her highly emotional state of mind at this time and how anxious she is at being parted from Romeo. It also reflects the importance she places on fate and fortune. The **personification** of fortune as a **'fickle'** (changeable) character who plays with people for her own amusement reflects Elizabethan views of fate. Juliet is refering here to Fortuna, the goddess of luck, who kept a wheel that determined one's happiness. A person could be at the top of the wheel, enjoying health and prosperity, but if Fortuna chose to spin her wheel, then life could change dramatically. Juliet sees fate as having control over Romeo, being able to **'send'** him places on a whim (fancy).

☑ Make the point that Juliet's fate is bound up with the fate of Verona

Juliet's unease and uncertainty are shown in the use of the question **'all men call thee fickle: If thou art fickle, what dost thou with him/ That is renown'd for faith?'** The **repetition** of **'fickle'** shows she is aware of how quickly events can change. The use of **'faith'** with **'fickle'** shows oppostite ideas and reflects one of the themes of the play, that of contrasting forces that need to be balanced and reconciled. It is only through the lovers living out their fate and dying for love that peace comes to Verona.

☑ Move to the start of the play to show how fate sets out the lovers' paths

In the Prologue, the chorus warns us that Romeo and Juliet are **'star-cross'd'**, that there is nothing they can do to escape their fate of death. The chorus is a device used by ancient Greek playwrights and by Shakespeare to guide the audience response. By having this foreknowledge that the lovers will die, we are constantly aware of the relentless presence of fate throughout the play, and are implicitly involved in the couple's doomed relationship. This creates constant tension and unease: an effective dramatic device. Also, by telling us the ending of the play, the audience is aware from the very beginning that they will be watching a story of pain, conflict and death; it is a compelling and dramatic opening. **Images** associating Juliet with light weave through the play such as **'bright angel'** and **'she doth teach the torches to burn bright'**. These **images** constantly remind the audience that she is **'star-cross'd'**, creating a sense of unease. Astrology, consulting the stars to see what the future would hold, was very popular in the Elizabethan era. The audience would have believed that the alignment (positioning) of the stars meant that the lovers were doomed.

☑ Explore an alternative view of fate

Yet it is perhaps unfair to blame fate entirely for the tragedy. Romeo's reaction to hearing about Juliet's death is one of despairing defiance as he shouts **'then I defy you, stars!'** He addresses the cold, unfeeling powers that govern his life and cause such grief; he recognises that fate has played its part in Juliet's death but decides to show his own power. By killing himself, he is taking back the last vestige of control, choosing his own place and time of death. Yet if Romeo had not been so hasty, if he had waited a few moments, then tragedy could have been averted. Shakespeare uses the Greek conventions of tragedy which means that the tragic hero, Romeo, has a **hamartia** (fatal flaw) which leads to his downfall; it is this fatal flaw of impetuousness that results in the lovers' deaths. However, fate's control of the situation and characters is also clear. From the beginning, the Prologue warns us that the lovers are **'star-cross'd'** and therefore doomed to die. There is nothing Romeo could do to avert his fate; by choosing suicide as his course of action, he merely plays into the hands of fate, becoming the first of the **'star-cross'd lovers'** to die. This adds to the overwhelming sense of tragedy and that the death of the lovers is inevitable.

14 Conflict
Exploration of a theme

Conflict is a theme which runs throughout the play, reflecting the era in which Shakespeare was writing. The Renaissance period was a time of great political turmoil and also a time when Medieval ideas were being challenged by art and science. The idea of conflict is deeply embedded in the play.

'Peace? I hate the word as I hate hell, all Montagues and thee'

- In Act 1, Tybalt and Benvolio represent two ideas in conflict with each other- violence and peace.

- There is clear **juxtaposition** between Benvolio's desire to keep the peace and Tybalt's desire to destroy it, and the language here captures that.

- Tybalt rejects peace with the **repetition** of the **verb 'hate'**, showing his angry nature. The short, **monosyllabic** statement makes it very clear how passionately he is linked to violence and infected with the hatred that dominates the play.

- Tybalt's words link hell and Montagues, a dark link that associates Montagues with the devil. This is an irrational (no logic or sense) hatred and deeply corrosive (damaging).

- This opening scene is visually one of physical conflict as the street brawl erupts and the language also captures the conflict.

'these violent delights have violent ends'

- Friar Lawrence and Romeo show the **contrast** between youth and age. There is conflict between the impetuousness (quick decision-making) of youth and the wisdom that age brings.

- The Friar sees young love as dangerous and this is highlighted in the **repetition** of **'violent'**. It **foreshadows** the end of the play when Romeo's hasty decision-making does indeed lead to tragedy.

- Yet there is not always wisdom in age. Lord Capulet shows foolishness as he rushes around for a sword to join in the fighting. Shakespeare uses humour here as Lady Capulet, who is much younger, mocks him, calling **'a crutch! A crutch! Why call you for a sword?'** to highlight the folly (silliness) of his actions. This shows that the conflict between age and youth is complicated as the older figures do not always demonstrate the wisdom they should.

'turn your households' rancour to pure love'	• This is a clear **statement** of intent; the Friar wants the love of Romeo and Juliet to act as a way of healing the rift between the two houses. From the beginning, he is seen as a healer and his reasons for trying to help them are for the greater good of Verona and to put an end to the violence. His **contrasting** words **'rancour'** (meaning animosity or dislike) and **'love'** highlight this theme of the play, that of conflict and the need to bring balance and harmony. • It is ironic that the lovers' marriage does indeed result in an end to the rivalry but through death, certainly not as the Friar planned. This shows how fate cannot be controlled and changed.

'make blessed my rude hand'

• Romeo sees himself as profane (not religious) but blesses himself when he touches Juliet's hand upon first meeting her. This shows the conflict between the profane and the sacred in the play.

• Juliet is constantly seen as pure and sacred with religious *imagery* such as **'bright angel'** used to describe her. Romeo is seen as more down-to-earth. This is reflected in the staging of the balcony scene when Juliet is above Romeo.

• The conflict between the profane and the secular is reconciled when Romeo and Juliet are married and so have the blessing of the Church. Yet their union is short-lived, showing how other forces in conflict with each other still conspire to destroy the couple.

Context: The Christian religion was a fundamental part of Elizabethan England. The religious imagery validates the pure nature of Romeo and Juliet's love. This means that when the couple commit suicide, seen as a serious sin by the Church, the audience still feels sympathy.

'hang, beg, starve, die'

• There is painful conflict within families when Juliet refuses to marry Paris and Capulet explodes with rage.

• The violent **verbs** Capulet uses show the extent of his rage. The **monosyllabic** words are spat out in vicious fury, and **structurally**, the final **verb** 'die' **foreshadows** the violence that will in part at least result from his fury.

Context: In Elizabethan England and in 14th century Italy, parents decided their children's wedding partners. Juliet's defiance would be shocking but for the fact the audience have been watching the blossoming of love between Romeo and Juliet.

> **'Call me but love, and I'll be new baptized'**

- Romeo tells Juliet he will give up his entire identity if she'll love him. This shows the conflict between the individual and society.

- This conflict between what society expects and what the individual wishes runs throughout the play. This is why Romeo and Juliet need to meet and love in secrecy, under cover of night, away from public view.

- Often Shakespeare uses **structure** to show this idea e.g. the **juxtaposition** between the private, peaceful wedding service and the heat of the public square that afternoon when tempers flare and Mercutio and Tybalt are killed.

Grade 9 Exploration:
Look at the theme in a different way

Does Shakespeare teach us that conflict can be resolved?

Yes: The Prince concludes the play with the lines **'for never was a story of more woe/Than this of Juliet and her Romeo'**. The **rhyming couplets** in this final speech help give the play a sense of **resolution** and conclusion as the feud and conflict is ended. It would have been a reassuring message for the Elizabethan audience at a time of great political, religious and economic turmoil.

No: Capulet promises to raise a statue for Romeo, saying **'as rich shall Romeo's by his lady's lie/Poor sacrifices of our enmity'** but he only mentions this because Montague states how he intends to raise a statue of pure gold for Juliet first. This is a clear attempt to upstage his old foe. It makes the audience wonder whether the feud is really settled and buried or whether there will be future conflict. Shakespeare is showing us that conflict is inevitable within human experience.

Essential Exam Tips

- ☑ Look at punctuation marks in the extract. Question marks indicate questions which suggest uncertainty and confusion. Exclamation marks suggest passion or violence or humour.

- ☑ Now you're at the end of this guide, you can see how easy it is to 'recycle' the same ideas. This should help you revise efficiently and effectively.

Conflict

The language **contrasts 'peace'** and **'hate'**, showing how deep and damaging the hate is.

↑

'Peace? I hate the word as I hate hell, all Montagues and thee'

↑

There is conflict between the two families.

The violent **monosyllabic verbs** are spat out by Lord Capulet, revealing the division between parent and child.

↑

'hang, beg, starve, die'

↑

There is conflict within families.

There is conflict between the individual and society.

↑

'Call me but love, and I'll be new baptized'

↑

Romeo is offering to give up his whole identity for love; he understands how Verona society will not allow his personal love to develop.

Is the conflict resolved?

↓

Yes: **'For never was a story of more woe/Than this of Juliet and her Romeo'.** The **rhyming couplets** in this final speech help give the play a sense of **resolution** as the conflict is ended.

↓

No: **'As rich shall Romeo's by his lady's lie/Poor sacrifices of our enmity'**

At the end, Capulet seems to be still concerned about his status against the Montagues and not his daughter. Conflict between the families continues.

Sample GCSE Exam Question

Read the following extract from Act 1 Scene 5 of 'Romeo and Juliet'.

Answer both questions below the text.

At this point in the play, Tybalt has just spotted Romeo at the Capulets' party and wishes to fight him.

TYBALT:
'Tis he, that villain Romeo.

CAPULET:
Content thee, gentle coz, let him alone;
He bears him like a portly gentleman;
And, to say truth, Verona brags of him
To be a virtuous and well-govern'd youth:
I would not for the wealth of all the town
Here in my house do him disparagement:
Therefore be patient, take no note of him:
It is my will, the which if thou respect,
Show a fair presence and put off these frowns,
And ill-beseeming semblance for a feast.

TYBALT:
It fits, when such a villain is a guest:
I'll not endure him.

CAPULET:
He shall be endured:
What, goodman boy! I say, he shall: go to;
Am I the master here, or you? go to.
You'll not endure him! God shall mend my soul!
You'll make a mutiny among my guests!
You will set cock-a-hoop! you'll be the man!

a) Discuss how conflict is presented in this extract.

b) Discuss how conflict is presented in the play as a whole.

Sample GCSE Answer

 Start with an overview

Conflict is a theme which runs throughout the play, reflecting the era in which Shakespeare was writing. The Renaissance period was a time of great political turmoil and also a time when Medieval ideas were being challenged by art and science. The idea of conflict is deeply embedded in the play, and in this scene we witness family divisions as Tybalt defies his uncle and seeks out physical confrontation.

 Make the point that even as Romeo is falling in love, there is violence and conflict

Tybalt calls Romeo a **'villain'**, an unpleasant insult in Elizabethan England which the audience would have recognised as being inflammatory. His language also reveals his intention of violence as he says **'I'll not endure him'**. The *modal verb* **'will'** reflects the certainty and commitment to the violence he intends. This language

foreshadows the fighting in Act 3 when Tybalt dies and the tragic series of events are triggered. It also sharply **juxtaposes** with the beautiful **metaphors** that Romeo used moments before with **'she doth teach the torches to burn bright!'** as he falls in love with Juliet. This shows the audience how, even at moments of great romance, there is also dark conflict.

✓ Make the point that Capulet does try to keep the peace and resolve the conflict

Capulet tries to placate (calm down) Tybalt, telling him **'content thee, gentle coz, let him alone'**. His language is conciliatory (peaceful) as he addresses him with the warm **epithet 'gentle coz'**. This **epithet** appeals to both Tybalt's nobility with **'gentle'**, and also the ties and loyalty of family with **'coz'** (which means 'cousin'). Interestingly, Capulet is able to see the good in Romeo despite the families' conflict, calling him **'a virtuous and well-govern'd youth'**. This is heartening; perhaps Shakespeare was showing the Elizabethan audience, when great political and social turmoil threatened them, that human nature can be forgiving and accepting.

✓ Make the point that Capulet fails to resolve the conflict and in fact escalates it

Yet despite Capulet's efforts, Tybalt refuses to back down and Capulet's hasty temper explodes as he demands **'am I the master here, or you? go to.'** Capulet's status as head of the household has been challenged and this is reflected in the question that demands Tybalt acknowledge his authority. Social status was rigidly held to in the Elizabethan era, and the audience would have appreciated Capulet's demand to be respected and obeyed. His anger reminds us that, although he is older and should be wiser, his temper is sometimes uncontrollable; in the first scene, he demands his sword, calling **'give me my long sword'**. The **imperative verbs 'give'** and then **'go'** in this extract create his sense of authority; this authority is abused to escalate the conflict. And here conflict within the family is shown through Capulet's language which changes from the pleasant use of **'thee'** to the much ruder **'you'**.

✓ Move to another part of the play to show how conflict is shown between religious and profane

Romeo sees himself as profane (not religious) but improves himself and blesses himself when he touches Juliet's hand upon first meeting her, saying **'make blessed my rude hand'**. This shows the conflict between the profane and the the sacred in the play. Juliet is constantly seen as pure with religious **imagery** such as **'bright angel'** used about her. Romeo is portrayed as more down-to-earth and this is reflected in the staging of the balcony scene when Juliet is above Romeo. The conflict between the profane and the secular is reconciled when Romeo and Juliet are married and so have the blessing of the Church. Yet their union is very short-lived, perhaps showing how other forces in conflict with each other still conspire to destroy the couple. The Christian religion was a fundamental part of Elizabethan England and the religious **imagery** validates the pure nature of Romeo and Juliet's love. This means that when the couple commit suicide, seen as a serious sin by the Church, the audience still sympathises with the tragic couple.

✓ Move to the end of the play and explore whether conflict has been resolved

Conflict seems to be resolved at the end as the Prince concludes the play with the lines **'for never was a story of more woe/Than this of Juliet and her Romeo'**. The **rhyming couplets 'woe/Romeo'** in this final speech help give the play a sense of **resolution** and conclusion as the feud and conflict is ended. It would have been a reassuring message for the Elizabethan audience at a time of great political, religious, social and economic turmoil. Yet the conflict does perhaps linger; Capulet promises to raise a statue for Romeo, saying **'as rich shall Romeo's by his lady's lie/Poor sacrifices of our enmity'** but he only mentions this because Montague states how he intends to raise a statue of pure gold for Juliet first. This is a clear attempt to upstage his foe. It makes the audience wonder whether the feud is really settled and buried or whether there will be future conflict. Shakespeare is perhaps showing us that conflict is inevitable within human experience and that the conflict which leads to such tragedy will be repeated many thousands of times over.

Quotations
Recap & Revise

The Prologue

'A pair of star-cross'd lovers take their life'
The chorus warns us that this is a tragedy.

Act 1 Scene 1

'I do but keep the peace'
Benvolio tries to stop the street fight.

'Peace? I hate the word, as I hate hell, all Montagues and thee'
Tybalt wants to escalate the violence.

'Give me my long sword, ho!'
Lord Capulet joins in the street fight.

'A crutch! A crutch! Why call you for a sword?'
Lady Capulet teases her old husband for wanting to fight.

'pain of torture'
The Prince threatens violence to the fighting men.

'Throw your mistempered weapons'
The Prince orders both families to disarm.

'Three civil brawls......have thrice disturbed the quiet of our streets'
The Prince is angry at the violence in the street.

'cankered with peace, to part your cankered hate'
The Prince rebukes the families for their fighting.

'Your lives shall pay the forfeit of the peace'
The Prince warns the families that future violence will be punished with death.

'O brawling love, O loving hate!'
Romeo shows his horror at the street fight.

'She'll not be hit/With Cupid's arrow, she hath Diana's wit'
Romeo speaks adoringly of how unattainable the perfect Lady Rosaline is.

'I weep... at thy good heart's oppression'
Benvolio shows compassion for Romeo's sadness.

Act 1 Scene 2

'And too soon marred are those so early made'
Lord Capulet comments that girls can be damaged if married too early.

'Hopeful lady of my earth'
Lord Capulet shows his affection for Juliet.

'Woo her, gentle Paris, get her heart'
Lord Capulet wants Juliet to marry Paris for love.

'I am sent to find these persons whose names here are writ'
The servant giving out the invitations to the Capulets' party cannot read.

'prettiest babe that ever I nursed'
The Nurse breast-fed Juliet.

Act 1 Scene 3

'Not fourteen'
Juliet is only thirteen years old.

'Madam, I am here. What is your will?'
Juliet starts the play addressing her mother with great respect and formality.

'Susan is with God/She was too good for me'
The Nurse speaks with acceptance about her own baby's death.

'So shall you share all that he doth possess'
Lady Capulet tries to convince Juliet that Paris is a good match.

'I'll look to like, if looking liking move'
Juliet tells her mother that she will try to like Paris.

Act 1 Scene 4

'that dreamers often lie'
Mercutio teases Romeo about his dreams.

'Queen Mab ...plagues with blisters'
Mercutio describes Queen Mab, the bringer of dreams.

Act 1 Scene 5

'O she doth teach the torches to burn bright!'
Romeo is overwhelmed by Juliet's beauty.

'Make blessed my rude hand'
Romeo sees himself as being blessed when he touches Juliet's hand.

'I'll not endure him'/'He shall be endured'
Tybalt is furious at Romeo's intrusion to the ball but Lord Capulet tells him to back down.

'If he be married/My grave is like to be my wedding bed'
When Juliet meets Romeo, she falls instantly in love.

Act 2 Scene 1

'That she were an open-arse, thou a pop'rin pear'
Mercutio makes rude jokes.

Act 2 Scene 2

'Bright angel'
Romeo shows a respectful attitude to Juliet.

'Call me but love, and I'll be new baptized'
Romeo tells Juliet he will give up his entire identity if she'll love him.

'Too rash, too unadvised, too sudden'
On the balcony, Juliet questions the intensity and wisdom of their love.

Act 2 Scene 3

'day/night' 'baleful weeds/precious-juiced flowers'
Friar Lawrence is a holy man who is linked to Nature.

'Pupil mine/young son'
The Friar shows his closeness to Romeo.

'Turn your households' rancour to pure love'
The Friar wants the marriage to put an end to the families' rivalry.

Act 2 Scene 4

'Switch and spurs, switch and spurs; or I'll cry a match'
Romeo brings his witty verbal sparring to an end.

Act 2 Scene 5

'I am weary, give me leave a while'
The Nurse pretends to be tired, delaying telling Juliet about the marriage plans.

'O honey nurse'
Juliet address her Nurse with positive affection.

'You shall bear the burden soon at night'
The Nurse uses wordplay to make crude sexual reference to Juliet's wedding night.

Act 2 Scene 6

'These violent delights have violent ends'
Friar Lawrence warns of the explosive nature of love.

'Holy Church incorporate two as one'
The Friar marries Romeo and Juliet.

Act 3 Scene 1

'The day is hot, the Capulets are abroad'
Benvolio warns that trouble is coming.

'Boy, this shall not excuse the injuries'
Tybalt holds onto his grudge.

'O calm dishonourable vile submission'
Mercutio cannot understand Romeo's refusal to fight Tybalt.

'Tomorrow you shall find me a grave man'
Mercutio makes jokes even as he dies.

'A plague a'both your houses'
Mercutio's final words curse both the Montagues and the Capulets.

'Fire-eyed fury be my conduct now'
Romeo is motivated by anger and revenge after Mercutio is killed.

'stout Mercutio...stout Tybalt'
Benvolio gives a fair account of the fight.

'I have an interest in your hearts' proceedings'
The Prince admits he has a personal

involvement in the families' feuding.

'Romeo slew Tybalt, Romeo must not live'
Lady Capulet calls for Romeo's death sentence.

Act 3 Scene 2

'Spread they close curtain, love-performing night'
Juliet is impatient for her wedding night.

Act 3 Scene 5

'As one dead in the bottom of a tomb'
Juliet looks down at Romeo and has a vision that he is dead.

'O fortune...all men call thee fickle'
Juliet sees Fortune and Fate as controlling and unreliable.

'I would the fool were married to her grave'
Lady Capulet rejects Juliet when she refuses to marry Paris.

'Does she not give us thanks?'
Lord Capulet is angry and confused that Juliet does not want to marry Paris.

'Out you baggage! You tallow-face!'
Lord Capulet insults Juliet when she refuses to marry Paris.

'Hang, beg, starve, die'
Lord Capulet curses his daughter when she disobeys him.

'You are to blame, my lord, to rate her so'
The Nurse tries to defend Juliet to Lord Capulet.

'Beshrew my very heart, I think you are happy in this second match'
The Nurse advises Juliet to forget her

husband and obey her parents by marrying Paris.

Act 4 Scene 1

'O bid me leap, rather than marry Paris... from off the battlements'
Juliet claims that she would rather kill herself than marry Paris.

Act 4 Scene 5

'O day O day O hateful day!'
The Nurse reacts with violent grief to the discovery of Juliet's body.

'Our wedding cheer to a sad burial feast'
Lord Capulet is horrified when he finds his daughter dead on her wedding morning.

Act 5 Scene 1

'Then I defy you, stars!'
Romeo hears of Juliet's 'death' and shouts defiance at Fate.

'violently as hasty powder fired'
When he hears of the 'death' of Juliet, Romeo seeks a swift death himself by drinking deadly poison.

Act 5 Scene 3

'I dare no longer stay'
The Friar deserts Juliet in the tomb.

'Unkind hour'
The Friar blames Fate for the tragic deaths.

'winking at your discords'
The Prince says that he has turned a blind eye to the feud.

'All are punished'
The Prince acknowledges that all have been hurt by the tragedy.

'As rich shall Romeo's by his lady's lie/ Poor sacrifices of our enmity'
Lord Capulet promises to pay for a statue of Romeo to match the statue of Juliet.

'The sun for sorrow will not show its head'
The Prince sees the scale of the tragedy- even the sun is mourning.

'For never was a story of more woe/Than this of Juliet and her Romeo'
The Prince states how tragic the lovers' deaths are.

Glossary
Explanation of terms

ADJECTIVE - a word that describes a noun **e.g. 'gallant man'**

ADVERB - a word that describes a verb **e.g. 'Immediately we exile him hence'**

ALLITERATION - repetition of the same letter in words next to or near each other **e.g. 'Fire-eyed fury'**

ANECDOTE - a personal story **e.g. the Nurse tells stories of Juliet as a baby**

BLANK VERSE - type of poetry

CATHARSIS - an emotional release after great tension

COMIC RELIEF - humorous moment that eases tension **e.g. Mercutio jokes as he is dying**

COMMAND VERB - see **imperative verb**

CONJUNCTION - word to connect two clauses or phrases e.g. 'Yes madam; yet I cannot choose but laugh'

CONTRAST/ JUXTAPOSITION - use of opposites **e.g. the quiet harmony of the wedding scene is directly followed by the violent conflict of the fight scene**

DRAMATIC IRONY - when the audience knows something the characters do not **e.g. only the audience understands Romeo's refusal to fight**

EPITHET - an adjective attached to a proper noun. Used to describe a person **e.g. 'honey nurse'**

EXCLAMATORY SENTENCE - sentence that ends with an exclamation mark **e.g. 'O she doth teach the torches to burn bright!'**

EXTENDED METAPHOR/ CONCEIT - when a metaphor is developed **e.g. Lady Capulet uses an extended metaphor of a book to describe Paris**

FOIL - something or someone that works as a contrast **e.g. Mercutio's view of love works as a foil against Romeo's**

FORESHADOWING - to give a warning of a future event **e.g. 'these violent delights have violent ends'**

HAMARTIA - convention from Greek tragedy where the noble and tragic hero has a fatal flaw **e.g. Romeo's harmartia is his tendency to act without thinking.**

HYPERBOLE - exaggerated words or phrases **e.g. 'O bid my leap from the battlements!'**

Iambic pentameter - 10 syllables to a line

IMAGE/IMAGERY - powerful words or phrase that paints a picture in our heads **e.g. 'bright angel' uses religious imagery to describe Juliet**

IMPERATIVE VERB - verb that gives an order **e.g. 'Spread they close curtain'**

JUXTAPOSITION - see contrast

INTERJECTION - an added word or phrase **e.g. 'Give me my long sword, ho!'**

MAJESTIC PLURAL PRONOUN - plural pronoun used by an individual of high rank **e.g. The Prince says 'we do exile him hence'**

METAPHOR - desciding a person or object as something else **e.g. 'O she doth teach the torches to burn bright!'**

MINOR SENTENCE - a sentence not grammatically complete **e.g. 'O fortune, fortune'**

MODAL VERBS - verbs that show a level of certainty **e.g. 'I will be deaf to pleadings'**

MONOSYLLABIC - words of one syllable **e.g. 'Thus with a kiss I die'**

NOUN - name of an object/place/time/emotion **e.g. Romeo or 'villain'**

NOUN PHRASE - words that go with a noun **e.g. 'whining mammet'**

OXYMORON - words that reveal a paradox or contradiction **e.g. 'brawling love'**

PATHETIC FALLACY - when weather reflects the character's mood **e.g. 'hot' day in the fight scene**

PATHOS - sadness

PATRIARCHAL - a society where men are dominant/have power

PERSONAL PRONOUN - word that replaces a proper noun **e.g. 'I' or 'He' rather than 'The Prince'**

PERSONIFICATION - when an object is given human qualities **e.g. 'The sun, for sorrow, will not show his head'**

PETRARCHAN LANGUAGE - the overly romantic language used to worship a lady

PLOSIVE - hard sound made by a consonant 'd' 'b' 't' 'p' 'k' **e.g. 'she doth teach the torches to burn bright'**

PLOT DEVICE - technique used to move the story along

POSSESSIVE PRONOUN - word that shows something belongs to someone **e.g. 'pupil mine'**

PROSE- ordinary speech rather than poetry/blank verse

PUNS - jokes when a word has two meanings **e.g. 'ask for me tomorrow and you shall find me a grave man'**

REPETITION - when a word or phrase is repeated **e.g. 'O day O day!'**

RESOLUTION - the conclusion of a play when conflict is resolved

RHYMING COUPLETS - pair of lines that both end in the same rhyming sound **e.g. 'For never was there a story of more woe/Than that of Juliet and her Romeo'**

SEMANTIC FIELD - more than one word on a subject that builds up a theme **e.g. Friar Lawrence uses a semantic field of opposing contrasts 'day/night' and 'weeds/flowers'**

SETTING - where a scene is played out **e.g. the opening setting is in the streets of Verona**

SIMILE - describing a person or object as something else using 'like' or 'as' **e.g. 'violently as hasty powder fired'**

SITUATIONAL IRONY - when a situation results in the opposite result to what was intended **e.g. when the servant is supposed to be inviting the Capulets' friends to the party but invites the Montagues**

SOLILOQUY - a speech where the character speaks his/her thoughts aloud.

STATEMENT - a definite expression of something **e.g. 'All are punished'**

STRUCTURE - the order in which a line/scene/play is put together

SUSPEND DISBELIEF - when an audience stops questioning the realism of the story

SYMBOL - when an object/person stands for something else **e.g light is a symbol of hope**

TONE - mood or atmosphere

TRI-COLON - parallel phrase used 3 times **e.g. 'Too rash, too unadvised, too sudden'**

TRIPLET - list of three items **e.g. 'O calm dishounourable vile submission'**

VERB - an action word **e.g Capulet uses violent verbs such as 'hang, starve, die'**

VOCABULARY - words chosen by a character

VOWEL SOUNDS - sounds that vowels (aeiou) make. Long vowel sounds **e.g the long 'o' and 'a' in 'open arse'**

WORDPLAY - see **pun**

Lightning Source UK Ltd.
Milton Keynes UK
UKHW051204271222
414350UK00005B/25

9 781999 840242